Contents

List of figures

Coinage in the
Roman World

Index correlates plates with discussions in the text for Burnett's Coinage in the Roman World. *By Warren W. Esty*

Andrew Burnett's Coinage in the Roman World is an excellent introduction to Roman monetary history. It is well illustrated with photographs of 187 coins which are referenced in the text. Unfortunately, the list of illustrations only identifies the coins – it does not cite the pages on which the coins are discussed. This index provides those citations, as well as referencing those coins found in the tables on pages 4 and 12. It is suitable for photocopying and will fit nicely inside the back cover of the book. Similar indices for other volumes in this series of Seaby books will be forthcoming.

First published in *The Celator*, June 1991

Coin	Pages	Coin	Pages	Coin	Pages
1	3, 4, 8	63	19, 27, 54, 109	126	124, 142
2	3	64	55	127	65
3	3, 4, 5, 6	65	19, 62	128	141, 142
4	4, 5	66	58, 81, 82, 84	129	142
5	1, 4	67	55, 75	130	45, 87, 128
6	3, 4, 5, 12	68	44	131	142, 143
7	3, 4, 5, 16	69	45, 87	132	142, 143
8	4, 12, 16, 143	70	51	133	143
9	4, 5, 8	71	18	134	127, 143
10	5, 8	72	75	135	127, 143
11	4, 5, 8	73	75, 78	136	128, 131, 143
12	8	74	37, 55, 109	137	129
13	4, 6, 12	75	37, 56, 97	138	143
14	4, 6	76	84	139	144
15	4, 6, 34	77	43, 87	140	67, 68, 145
16	4, 6	78	76	141	129, 146
17	21, 22, 34, 71	79	50, 76	142	145
18	21, 34, 35, 71	80	43, 87	143	131
19	21, 34, 35, 71	81	46	144	116, 131
20	21, 35, 71	82	25, 70, 75, 76	145	132, 146
21	21, 22, 34, 36, 71	83	57, 76	146	132, 144
22	22, 36	84	85	147	132, 144
23	22	85	67	148	68, 146
24	34, 36, 109	86	76	149	145
25	21, 35, 40	87	57, 76, 109, 155	150	134, 139, 144, 145
26	23	88	48, 70, 76	151	133, 144
27	22, 23, 99	89	48	152	133, 144
28	23, 24	90	58, 76, 109	153	133, 144
29	20, 22, 71	91	60, 67, 85	154	133
30	23, 100	92	76	155	133
31	23	93	42, 76, 87	156	147
32	21	94	57	157	129
33	72	95	109	158	68, 134, 137, 144
34	21	96	58, 83, 109	159	135
35	100	97	83	160	135
36	37, 39, 87	98	77, 79, 109	161	115, 137
37	51	99	84	162	137, 144
38	37, 40	100	77	163	138
39	40	101	48, 77	164	148
40	24, 40	102	84	165	135, 144, 147
41	24, 52, 80	103	60	166	138
42	24, 41, 80, 87	104	49	167	138
43	24, 43, 80, 81	105	(not referenced) see p.43	168	150
44	29, 49	106	47	169	147
45	19, 72, 76	107	30, 87	170	148, 150
46	24, 41, 68, 72	108	31, 87	171	150, 157
47	36, 52	109	31, 79	172	147, 148, 150, 156
48	36, 37, 52, 80	110	45	173	148, 150
49	37, 97	111	85	174	148
50	42, 87	112	32	175	154
51	43	113	32	176	150
52	53	114	49, 77	177	155
53	80	115	84	178	155
54	72, 73	116	64	179	155
55	19, 71, 73	117	84	180	158
56	73, 100	118	84	181	154
57	42, 73, 74, 87	119	63, 64, 122	182	158
58	74, 75	120	122, 124, 142	183	157
59	19, 53, 62	121	77, 122, 142	184	157
60	19, 27, 54	122	123, 124	185	158
61	27, 54	123	124	186	158
62	27, 54	124	124	187	159
		125	124		

Coinage in the
Roman World

Andrew Burnett

SPINK

LONDON

© Andrew Burnett 1987
First published 1987
Reprinted 2004

Typeset by Progress Filmsetting Ltd, EC1
and Printed in Great Britain by
Cromwell Press
Trowbridge
Wiltshire
for the publishers

Spink & Son Ltd
69 Southampton Row
Bloomsbury
London WC1B 4ET

ISBN 0 900652 85 3

Preface

Yes, another introduction to Roman coins. Still, the subject moves on. Every generation changes its preoccupations and interests. In this book, three guiding principles are important. Firstly, it aims to move away from just describing the coins to giving some historical explanation of them. Secondly, it aims to integrate the coinage of the eastern provinces, traditionally abandoned to the last chapter of books on "Greek" coins. Thirdly, a child of its times, it aims to treat coins as economic objects, by explaining both how and why they circulated, and how they can illuminate economic history. These aims are ambitious, and have only been partly attained, both because of the limited space available and the complexity of the subjects involved.

I should like to thank friends and colleagues for their help. I would single out Ian Carradice and, particularly, Roger Bland, who has saved me from many errors of fact and horrors of style. My thanks also to my parents, amongst other things for introducing me to the world of the word processor, and to my family, for putting up with my bad moods during the painful process of writing.

Andrew Burnett

Note on written sources

A number of passages from ancient literature have been quoted in this book. These may not be familiar to all readers of the book, and fall into different groups. The first group consists of works of literature or history. These have been referred to by the name of the author and, if he wrote more than one work which has survived, the title of the relevant work, sometimes abbreviated. Translations of the full text of these authors can nearly always be found in the series of volumes in the Loeb Classical Library. A number, such as Livy, Suetonius, Cicero or Tacitus, are also available in Penguin Classics.

The second group consists of inscriptions and papyri. Inscriptions are referred to by the name of the modern corpus in which they appear. These are:

CIL	=	*Corpus Inscriptionum Latinarum*
ILS	=	H. Dessau, *Inscriptiones Latinae Selectae*, and
OGIS	=	W. Dittenberger, *Orientis Graeci Inscriptiones Selectae*.

A few more recent inscriptions are cited from their publication in the *Journal of Roman Studies* (or *JRS*). For papyri, references are given to the standard publication, arranged by location or collection:

POxy	=	B.P. Grenfell, A.S. Hunt *et al.*, *The Oxyrhynchus Papyri*,
PRyl	=	A.S. Hunt *et al.*, *Catalogue of the Greek Papyri in the Rylands Library, Manchester*,
PBeattyPanop	=	T.C. Skeat, *Papyri from Panopolis in the Beatty Library, Dublin*.

Some papyri have been conveniently reprinted in the Loeb classical library under the title *Select Papyri*.

Finally, a number of laws are cited from the collection put together by Theodosius II and published in 448, known as the Theodosian Code (or *CTh*), using the edition published by T. Mommsen, P.M. Meyer and P. Krueger, *Codex Theodosianus*. Citations usually take the form of a reference followed by a date, which is the year in which the law was passed.

PART ONE

Chapter One

The adoption of coinage

Introduction

Rome made her first coins only in about 300 BC, some four and a half centuries after the traditional date of her foundation (753 BC). Previously the Romans had been familiar with the concept of money as a means of comparing values and had probably used a variety of goods as objects of money, as well as direct barter. Yet the Roman adoption of coinage seems surprisingly late, when we consider that coinage had been used in the Greek world, with which Rome had many contacts, for some three centuries since its invention at the end of the seventh century BC.

In Italy, coinage had been produced by the Greek colonies of the south very soon after its start in Greece, and there was therefore a long tradition of coinage in Italy before Rome first began to issue coins. Silver and bronze were being minted at cities such as Naples and Taranto in particular, with substantial issues also from Velia, Heraclea, Metapontum (5), Thurii and Croton (see Fig. 1.1). All these mints produced coinage in very large quantities in the late fourth century to pay for the wars (and the mercenaries required to fight them) against the inland tribal peoples of Italy, who had been steadily encroaching on the position of the cities. The cities had hired a succession of foreign leaders and forces from Greece to help them; of these one of the most famous was Alexander the Molossian, cousin of Alexander the Great, who campaigned in Italy before 330 BC. After the turn of the century the Italian peoples were replaced by Rome as the main threat to the cities of the south, and to meet this threat they invited Pyrrhus, king of Epirus, to campaign in Italy on their behalf. After his failure in the Pyrrhic War (281–275 BC), Pyrrhus left Italy in the hands of Rome, but within a short time she came up against the power of Carthage, in the long naval First Punic War (264–241 BC) for control of Sicily. The decisive struggle between the two powers, the Second Punic War (218–201 BC), began with Hannibal's march across the Alps and ended with Carthage's defeat at the battle of Zama in Africa, leaving Rome the undisputed mistress of the western Mediterranean.

1

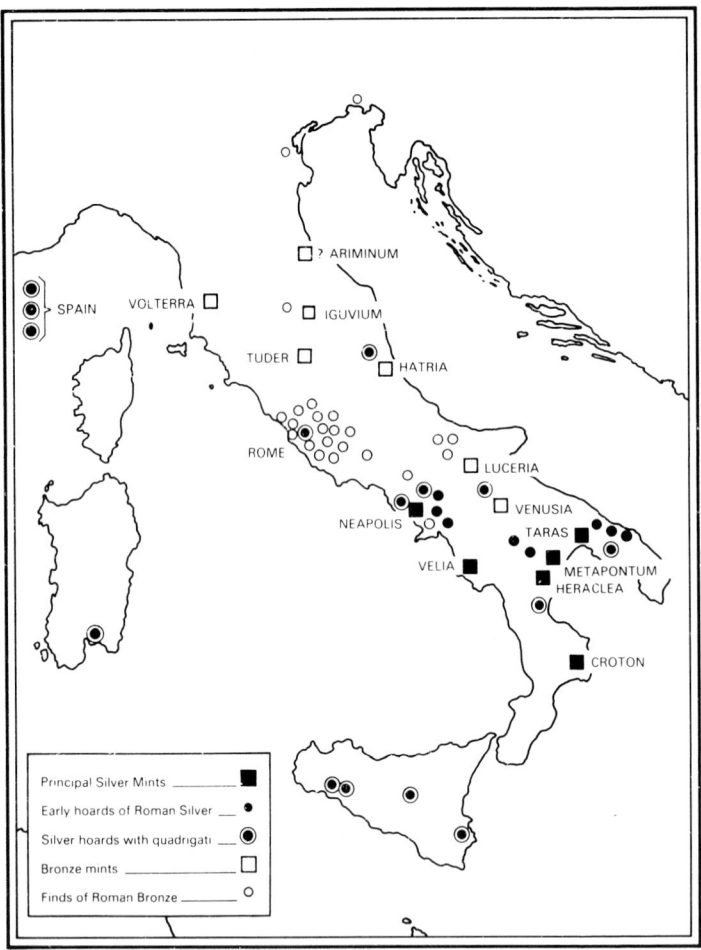

FIG. 1.1 Coinage in the Third Century BC

This is the period (about 300 BC to 210 BC) during which the first, so-called Romano-Campanian or pre-denarius, coinage was produced. Traditionally accounts of it have concentrated on the question of chronology – when exactly did coinage begin? This, of course, is an important question, not just for its intrinsic interest, but because, as will be seen, it appears to involve a clash between literary and numismatic evidence and because of the implications for the development of Roman society. This last consideration raises some of the other questions which may perhaps also be asked of the coinage of the period. What was it for? Why was it adopted? Why was it adopted at that particular time? What, if anything, does it tell us of Rome's economic, political or cultural development?

Description and structure

The early Roman coinage is quite unlike that of any other ancient society, since it combined a number of unusual elements, summarised in Fig. 1.2. There were four of these: the large bronze bars or bricks now known as 'aes signatum' (1); the struck silver and struck bronze coins (6, 7) with which we are familiar from Greek coinage, and the large bronze discs or coins, 'aes grave' (3).

The large bronze bars are known today as 'aes signatum' or 'struck bronze': (1). This name, though convenient, has no ancient authority, and is particularly inappropriate as the bars were cast in moulds rather than struck from dies. The bars are very large, measuring about 160 mm by 90 mm and weighing about 1500 to 1600 grams, that is to say, they apparently had a weight standard of about five Roman pounds. Today they are quite rare, but they have been found in hoards in and near Rome. Their presence in hoards and the references by ancient writers to the growing use of metal as money in Rome from the fifth century onwards make it clear that they had a monetary function, even though to our way of thinking they must have been incredibly inconvenient (a view which might also have been shared by later Romans, to judge from the stories in Livy about early Roman senators carrying their wealth around in waggons). They would not, however, have seemed so surprising to contemporaries, since the main form of money in central Italy at that time was metal valued according to its weight, as can be seen from archaeological finds and literary references. Moreover, the immediate predecessors of these Roman bars can be found in certain other Italian currency bars, the so-called 'ramo secco' or 'dry branch' bars (2), which were predominantly of northern Etruscan origin. They were first made in the sixth century BC and continued to be in use until the third century, when they were sometimes hoarded with Roman bars, thus demonstrating their common function. These ramo secco bars, however, differed from the Roman bars in several respects. In the first place, they were made of unrefined metal with a high iron content, whereas the Roman bars consisted of the highly leaded tin bronze so common in the Greek world at this time. Secondly, the design of the ramo secco bars was unchanging, whereas the designs of the

3

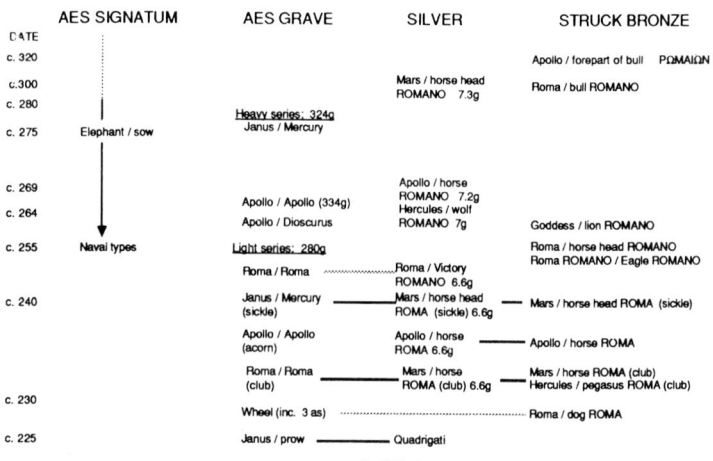

DATE	AES SIGNATUM	AES GRAVE	SILVER	STRUCK BRONZE
c. 320				Apollo / forepart of bull PΩMAIΩN
c.300			Mars / horse head ROMANO 7.3g	Roma / bull ROMANO
c. 280				
c. 275	Elephant / sow	Heavy series: 324g Janus / Mercury		
c. 269			Apollo / horse ROMANO 7.2g	
c. 264		Apollo / Apollo (334g) Apollo / Dioscurus	Hercules / wolf ROMANO 7g	Goddess / lion ROMANO
c. 255	Naval types	Light series: 280g Roma / Roma	Roma / Victory ROMANO 6.6g	Roma / horse head ROMANO Roma ROMANO / Eagle ROMANO
c. 240		Janus / Mercury (sickle)	Mars / horse head ROMA (sickle) 6.6g	Mars / horse head ROMA (sickle)
		Apollo / Apollo (acorn)	Apollo / horse ROMA 6.6g	Apollo / horse ROMA
		Roma / Roma (club)	Mars / horse ROMA (club) 6.6g	Mars / horse ROMA (club) Hercules / pegasus ROMA (club)
c. 230		Wheel (inc. 3 as)		Roma / dog ROMA
c. 225		Janus / prow	Quadrigati	

A solid line indicates a definite connection; a broken line a probable one

FIG. 1.2 *The Structure of the Early Roman Coinage*

Roman bars constantly changed, drawing on military and other, Italian, decorative themes. The designs had little obvious reference to Rome herself. Indeed only the similar shape of the bars and the geographical distribution of hoards which contain them, together with the occasional appearance of the inscription ROMANOM (= 'of the Romans' or 'Roman (bronze)'), demonstrate the Roman origin of the whole group. The third difference concerns weight. The ramo secco bars do not seem to have been made to any particular weight standard, whereas the Roman ones were (that of five pounds). This seems an important difference, representing a shift from objects made to be used as money in a general way to ones which were intended to play a specific role in a monetary system.

The second and third elements in the coinage were the struck silver and bronze coins, which differ little in appearance from the contemporary products of the Greek cities of southern Italy: for example, compare (6) with (5), the latter of Metapontum. Furthermore, both the method of manufacture and the weight standard were initially borrowed from the Greek-style coinage of nearby Naples. Only the use of a Latin legend, first ROMANO (6) and later ROMA (13), differentiates the Roman pieces from their Greek counterparts. Despite their similar appearance, however, the two metals had distinct functions and different areas of circulation (*see* Fig. 1.1). The bronze circulated mainly in central Italy together with the other two bronze elements of the coinage (the aes signatum and the aes grave), but the silver circulated mainly further south, particularly in Campania, hence the name Romano-Campanian. Moreover, at first, during the ROMANO phase of the coinage, bronze and silver seem to have been produced independently. There was no obvious relationship of weight between the coins of the two metals, and they also seem to have been made at different mints. With the exception of the first issue (6), which I think was probably made at Naples, all the silver was probably minted at Rome, whereas the early, ROMANO, bronze seems to have come from several different mints. Naples was probably the mint of the first two tiny issues, that with the Greek legend PWMAIWN (4) and that with a Neapolitan design on the reverse and the legend ROMANO. The plentiful issue with a head of Minerva on the obverse and a horse's head on the reverse (9) may have been minted at Cosa, the Latin colony lying on the coast some distance north or Rome (compare 10), while the large coins with a head of Roma or Minerva and an eagle (11) are nowadays found in Sicily, and were probably minted there during the First Punic War, perhaps at Palermo. Only the type with a head of a goddess and a lion (7) seems definitely to emanate from Rome itself. The earliest bronze therefore seems to consist of a number of different issues, varying widely in size, weight standard and mint.

The early silver, on the other hand, presents rather a different picture. Although the first issue was small in size, and isolated in date and perhaps mint, the rest of it was produced in a fairly steady and regular stream from a single mint at Rome.

The fourth element in the coinage is the so-called 'aes grave' or 'heavy bronze', which consisted of large round discs cast out of the same sort of bronze as the aes signatum (3). These coins were made in a number of denominations, based on the unit or 'as', which originally weighed a Roman pound (about 324 grams). These were:

unit	= as (3)	quarter	=	quadrans
half	= semis	sixth	=	sextans
third	= triens	twelfth	=	uncia

There are no obvious forerunners in Italy for the aes grave; it seems likely that the aes grave of other non-Roman communities was itself derived from the Roman model. It therefore seems reasonable to regard the Roman aes grave as an amalgam of the central Italian idea of a heavy metal currency with the south Italian idea of round coins.

Such were the four different elements of the coinage. How did they fit together? Fig. 1.1 has already illustrated that in some ways they did not. For instance, the bronze and silver had different areas of circulation, each being confined to an area with a tradition of currency in that particular metal. This differential circulation continued throughout most of the third century, even though later – in the period of the ROMA coinage – the different elements of the coinage were certainly produced together at the same place (Rome). This can be seen from the use of shared designs and letter forms, and most clearly from the use of the same symbols, like the sickle or club which appear on aes grave as well as struck silver and bronze (**13, 14, 3**). By this time the coinage was clearly integrated, with the three elements being made in parallel issues (the production of aes signatum ceased at about the end of the ROMANO phase). Moreover, by the time of this ROMA phase of the coinage, the weights of the different elements of the coinage had been adjusted to bring them into a close denominational relationship, so that there was an equation between one silver coin and three aes grave asses (the weights were adjusted to make this equation fit with the relative bullion value of bronze to silver, whereby silver was some 120 times more valuable than bronze). The final stage in this process of integration was that of design. There had already been a tendency to repeat the design used on one denomination or metal on another, and, at the very end of the period, with the issue of the 'quadrigati' (**15**), so-called from the quadriga or four-horse chariot on the reverse, all metals had a common obverse design with a janiform head, (**16**). This design was used also for the rare gold coins which were minted early in the Hannibalic War.

Before this, for the first generation or so of the coinage, the position is less clear, and it is only right to acknowledge that there is little agreement about this period. First, the denominational structure. There was probably no direct relationship at this time between the heavy bronze (aes signatum and aes grave) and the silver; rather both were independent, derived from different origins, and using weight standards which happened to be conveniently to hand (the Roman pound in one case and the weight standard of silver coins of Neapolis in the other). At this time the higher denomination corresponding to the as was not the silver, but the aes signatum bars, whose weight (five Roman pounds) was five times that of the as, to allow them to be five-as pieces. When the decision was made later to relate the silver and aes grave directly (by adjusting their weights so that 3 asses corresponded to one silver coin), the aes signatum's role was taken over by the silver, and this is why production of the aes signatum ceased precisely at this time.

This view of the lack of denominational structure in the Roman coinage at its inception is part of a more general view of the coinage as not beginning from some clearly planned initiative, but rather growing up as a collection of rather disparate elements produced more or less independently of each other. Later, weights were adjusted, minting was centralized and different denominations were produced according to a clear plan, but at this early date there were no such close links, whether of mint, weight standard or parallel production of different elements. The struck bronze was an irregular succession of issues, produced at several mints and on different weight standards. It was not produced in conjunction with the silver, which itself grew up in a rather haphazard way. The first small issue was probably made at Naples, on the Neapolitan weight standard; there was then a long gap, of some thirty years, until production resumed. During this period the heavy cast bronze coinage had been produced, but independently of the struck coinage.

Thus the early Roman coinage consisted initially of four separate elements, which sprang independently from their different origins, and were produced on a fairly fortuitous basis and on a rather restricted scale. Only after fifty years or so was the coinage overhauled and the links between the different elements systematised (a rationalisation which involved the abandonment of one of them, the aes signatum). This unification of the coinage was made clear by the use of common symbols on all the elements, and the final step was the adoption of a single obverse design (the janiform head) for all elements and metals: silver, bronze and eventually gold. This was the monetary system with which Rome entered the war against Hannibal (218–201 BC), and, but for the tremendous financial pressures exerted by the cost of the war, it might have survived for much longer. However, the huge costs of the war had a catastrophic effect on Rome's finances and coinage. The coinage was devalued in every way, by the reduction in weight standards of both bronze and silver, the sudden emergency production of gold coinage, and the debasement of the silver. All these measures were taken to make a limited stock of coinage metal go further than it could in paying the expenses of the war. Even these measures were insufficient, however, and it seems that for a short time the Roman state abandoned coinage altogether and lived on the credit of its private citizens (Livy 23.48.9, 24.11.7). Thus, in the field of coinage, Hannibal's legacy was the destruction of the original Roman coinage system. Subsequently, an entirely new start was made with the 'denarius system', which was to last for some four hundred years (*see* Part 2).

Dating

This description of the nature and structure of the early coinage has so far deliberately avoided giving dates, in view of the notorious modern controversy about its chronology. This controversy has existed mainly because of the difficulty in interpreting the literary evidence (especially that of Pliny) about the coinage, but also partly because of the inadequacy of the purely numismatic and archaeological evidence, which has been compatible with very different interpretations. Over the last few years, however, this position had greatly improved, mainly as a result of the discovery of new hoards. The study of these, together with other considerations such as the designs used, now allows us to approach the question of dating with greater confidence. First, let us consider the designs used. The fact that the designs of some early aes grave pieces are copied on Roman pottery made before 264 BC (*see* Fig. 1.3) clearly gives a date by which they have been produced. Again, the ROMANO bronzes from Sicily with an eagle on the reverse (**11**) copy coins of Ptolemaic Egypt (**12**), which also circulated in Sicily and which were minted in about 255 BC: this provides a date after which the Roman coins must have been made. Sometimes typology and history can be combined. For instance, Pyrrhus was the first commander to bring war elephants to Italy. These animals were so unfamiliar to the Romans that they did not know what to call them, so the appearance of one on an aes signatum bar (**1**) means that the bar can hardly have been produced before the period of the Pyrrhic War. Again, to judge from the close similarity of their designs, it seems that the bronzes with a head of Minerva or Roma and a horse's head (**9**) may have been minted in conjunction with the coinage with the same designs of the colony of Cosa (**10**). As Cosa was founded in 273 BC, the Roman coins are probably of a later date.

Thus an examination of the designs used can supply a number of useful chronological indications, but the evidence of coin hoards is potentially the more important. If we know the dates of the latest non-Roman coins in a mixed hoard of Roman and non-Roman coins, then that hoard can be dated by these non-Roman coins, and one can be fairly sure that the Roman coins in the hoard had been minted by that date. A series of such hoards, deposited at different dates, will theoretically reveal the detailed sequence of the coinage. Unfortunately, the hoards are not sufficiently numerous or satisfactorily recorded, except for those which include the first silver issue. Moreover, this approach obviously depends on the accuracy with which the

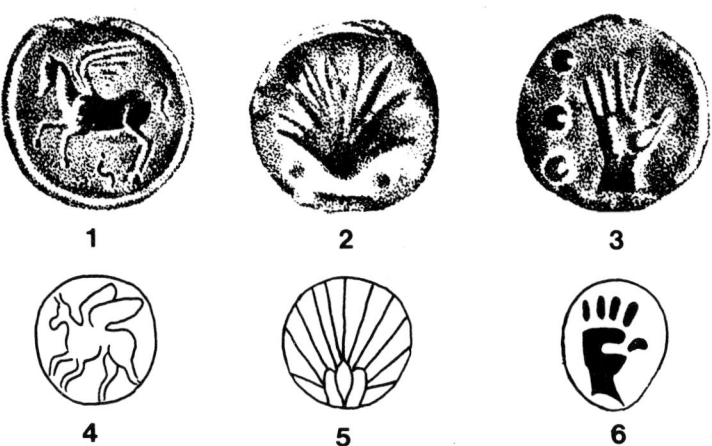

FIG. 1.3 *Pottery Stamps (4–6) copied from Aes Grave (1–3) (After J–P. Morel* MEFRA *1969, 107–8.)*

non-Roman coins can be dated, and there are only two good fixed points for these. Firstly, in the late fourth century a number of south Italian mints struck their coins on top of coins of Corinth. Sometimes this 'overstriking' was not done very carefully and the undertype can be identified. As the Corinthian coins can be fairly accurately dated, the overstrikes allow the relevant south Italian coins to be attributed with some confidence to about 335–330 BC. A century later, when the early Roman coins began to reach Sicily, they are sometimes found in hoards with coins which are explicitly signed as the products of King Hieronymus of Syracuse (215–214 BC), or the subsequent Syracusan democracy (214–212 BC). Everything between these two fixed points is rather less certain, but one can work out an intervening chronology for the non-Roman coins which is plausible and compatible with all the available hoard, typological and other non-literary evidence. On the basis of this framework, one can establish that the first issue of Roman silver was made in about 310–300 BC, followed by a long gap of some thirty years until the production of silver was restarted in about 270. From then it seems to have been fairly regularly minted until the Hannibalic War. The later coinage of the period was, as has been discussed, closely linked with the silver, so its dating can be automatically established from the silver; for the first period, however, there is little certainty. The dating of the beginning of the aes grave and aes signatum is very unclear – production may have started as early as the late fourth century, particularly in the case of the aes signatum, but it seems likely that the aes grave was not produced until the third century. Fig. 1.2 summarises the most probable current chronology of the period, in my opinion.

This chronology is based entirely on numismatic and archaeological evidence, but there is also some literary evidence about the beginning of the coinage, which appears to clash with the dating followed here. In Book XXXIII of his *Natural History*, Pliny, writing in the late first century AD, gave a potted history of Roman coinage from its beginnings.

"The Roman people did not even use coined silver before the defeat of Pyrrhus (281 BC.) . . . *King Servius* [traditionally dated 573–535 BC] *was the first to strike bronze.* Timaeus records that previously they used unworked bronze at Rome. It was stamped with the design of the 'pecus' [a cow], from which the name 'pecunia' [money] also comes. . . . Silver was struck in the 485th year of the city, when Q. Ogulnius and C. Fabius were consuls, five years before the first Punic War (264–241 BC). *And it was decided to value the denarius at 10 pounds of bronze, the quinarius at 5 and the sestertius at 2 pounds and a half.* Now the pound weight standard for bronze was reduced *during the First Punic War*, since the state could not meet its expenses, and it was decided that asses should be struck at a standard of one sixth of a pound. . . . Later, *when Hannibal was threatening and Q. Fabius Cunctator was dictator* (216 BC) asses of one ounce were made, and *it was decided to exchange a denarius for 16 asses.*" (*Natural History* 33.42–6.)

Pliny's date for the first silver coins is, according to all three methods he uses, 269 BC; he is drawing at least in part on an earlier source (Timaeus), and his date has the support of the main tradition of other ancient authors. Leaving aside Timaeus, who wrote in the third century BC, since we do not know exactly what he said, but have only Pliny's interpretation, the earliest occurrence of the date 269 seems to be from the reign of Augustus, since the historian Livy apparently included the story of the beginning of coinage in his work. The relevant part of Livy does not survive, but is known only from a much later summary which states, in the sentence after the foundation of a colony at Beneventum (268 BC), that "the Roman people then began to use silver". The tradition of a date in 269 or 268 was not, however, completely unanimous, since Varro, writing in the second century BC, apparently attributed some silver coins to the sixth-century king of Rome, Servius Tullius.

The literary evidence for the beginning of coinage in 269 or 268 BC has until recently formed the basis of the study of early Roman coinage. Until the middle of the twentieth century, the date of 269/8 was taken to be that of the introduction of the denarius, since Pliny talked of the denarius in the same breath as the beginning of silver coinage; the earlier – Romano-Campanian – coinage was thought to date from the fourth century BC. But, as it became clear that the denarius could not be so early, it was suggested that 269/8 was the date of the beginning of the first coinage. Nowadays, however, it is widely accepted that neither the inception of the early silver nor the denarius can be dated to 269/8, since the numismatic and archaeological evidence simply cannot be made compatible with either hypothesis, and various attempts have therefore been made to accommodate what Pliny says. Whether these attempts are really worth the effort is doubtful, as Pliny's remarks contain an astonishing number of mistakes and misdatings (italicised in the extract quoted). Whatever the quality of his sources, clearly not very much weight can be given to what he actually says. On the other hand, Timaeus, who was a contemporary of the third-century coinage, clearly said something about the coinage – and is it just coincidence that one of the few fragments of his work to have survived discussed the festival of the October Horse, which is alluded to on the first silver coin?. Thus there is reason to think that Pliny may have misrepresented some reliable statement about the beginning of the coinage.

Various explanations have been offered, of which the most popular sees 269/8 as the date at which a mint was established at Rome (Roman coins having previously been made elsewhere), at about the same time that other financial reforms were carried out: the number of quaestors or financial magistrates was increased in 267. This could be true, if, as is possible, the second issue of silver was dated then, since the first one was probably minted elsewhere, perhaps Naples. It is also possible, however, that what was recorded for 269 was simply the first distribution of booty in silver to the Roman populace. This is recorded by the Augustan source Dionysius of Halicarnassus as happening then (20.17), and it is noticeable that both Pliny and 'Livy' use the verb "use" rather than "strike". What may have been known was, for example, that in that year the first distribution of silver was made to the people; later this was taken to mean the first use of silver at Rome, and subsequently this was misunderstood to mean that silver was first minted in that year.

Function and purpose

What was the coinage for? Why was it adopted at Rome at all, and why in about 300 BC?

As a first stage in answering these questions, the scale of the coinage should be estimated, since any assessment of the function of the coinage must take into account the amount that was produced. The quantity of coinage produced in a given issue can be estimated by calculating the number of dies used to make it. This technique is discussed in greater detail in chapter five. By looking at the number of dies represented in a random sample, one can estimate the total number of dies used for the third-century coinage (before the quadrigati) as follows:

ROMANO coins

Type	observed dies	sample	estimated total dies
Mars	4	140	4
Apollo	10	70	10
Wolf + twins	33	199	35
Roma/Victory	35	206	37

ROMA coins

Mars/head	26	85	30
Apollo	26	108	29
Mars/horse	12	64	13

The table illustrates that the first issue was tiny in size in comparison with what came later, and that the scale of production gradually increased, reaching a peak in the middle of the third century, during the First Punic War, with the third and fourth ROMANO issues.

One can use the figures both to set the coinage against the little that we know of Roman finances and to compare it with the coinage of her great enemy, Carthage. Although we know almost nothing about the contemporary Roman state budget, we do have some figures about the value of spoil acquired by Rome in her various campaigns. First, Livy reports (10.39.6) that, in the triumph of Papirius Cursor in 293 BC, 1,830 pounds of silver were sent to Rome. This would have been enough silver for about 90,000 Roman silver coins, and, allowing an average output of some 30–40,000 coins per die (*see* chapter five), this figure is therefore of the same magnitude as the first Roman issue with its four obverse dies. Secondly, we know from an inscription that after the naval battle of Mylae in 260 BC the value of the spoils acquired by the Roman commander Duilius was somewhere between 2.9 and 3.4 million asses (the exact figure does not survive), the equivalent of around 27,000 pounds of silver. This amount of silver would have been enough to make about one and a quarter million coins of the wolf and twins type; as the total number of dies for this issue can be estimated at 35, one can conclude that the value of the silver minted was about the same as the value of the spoils captured at Mylae.

These 'statistics' are not used to suggest that the spoils of Papirius Cursor or of Duilius were made into these issues of coinage. Their purpose is rather to illustrate is that, relative to the size of her 'income', Rome's coinage was on a very small scale. Spoils were won on numerous other occasions, tribute was paid perhaps after the Pyrrhic and certainly after the First Punic War, yet the total silver output of Rome's coinage was only small in proportion to such revenue.

It seems that Roman coinage was also on a small scale relative both to that of her enemy Carthage and to that of contemporary Italian cities. The estimated number of dies used for the Roman coinage of the First Punic War, assuming that both the wolf and twins and the Roma/Victory coins were made then, was 72. The equivalent figure from contemporary Carthaginian silver, gold and electrum coins, allowing for the different weight standards used, was about 5,000. The amount of precious metal minted by Carthage during the First Punic War was then about 70 times as great as that of Rome.

The coinage of Rome was also small in comparison with that of the other south Italian mints. For instance, the mint of Heraclea, one of the medium-sized mints operating at the time, used some 60 dies for the coinage she produced during the Pyrrhic War; by that time the Roman coinage had consumed only some 14 dies, and over a much longer period. Later in the century one can use the representation of coins in hoards to demonstrate that the Roman coinage remained smaller than that of the two principal mints in south Italy, Naples and Taranto. Large issues of coinage tend to be well represented in hoards, smaller issues less so (*see* chapter five); and, although the hoard evidence from the middle of the third century is not very well recorded, one can see, for example in the hoards from Basilicata and Naples, that the Roman coinage of the period was produced on a much smaller scale than that of Naples and Taranto, although this difference has not been quantified.

The statistics, crude though they are, point firmly towards the conclusion that Roman coinage was small, when compared both to that of her contemporaries and to her own 'budget'. This consideration, combined with the picture of the structure outlined above, means that we must try to explain a coinage which was never very large, and began on a tiny scale, and which was, at first, produced only intermittently and in four different and unrelated forms. These factors mean it cannot have been used as the regular medium for military pay (a function which is generally agreed for the later denarius coinage), since, to pay soldiers, coinage must be produced regularly and in large enough quantities. Moreover the introduction of military pay at Rome (probably 406 BC, and certainly by 340 BC at the latest) preceded the introduction of coinage. Nor is there any correlation between the geographical distrubution of Roman coinage and military activity. Roman garrisons were established in several cities in Calabria (the toe of Italy) before the Pyrrhic War, but her coinage did not circulate there until two generations later; Rome acquired Sicily and Sardinia shortly after the First Punic War, but her coinage did not reach these islands before the Hannibalic War (*see* Fig. 1.1). Nevertheless, even if the coinage was not used for the regular payment of soldiers, it might have been used for some military purposes, for instance to repay the loans made by private citizens to build a fleet in 242 BC.

A number of further functions also seem likely, for instance paying for official dedications to the gods, which were at least sometimes financed by money collected in fines, and indeed funding other public works, such as the construction of roads like the via Appia. Indeed, if the suggestion that the coinage was at this time under the control of the censors is correct, then a function in the payment of public works, for which they were responsible, seems even more likely.

The early Roman coinage therefore probably had a number of different functions which are broadly speaking the same as those which were played by the contemporary coinage of southern Italy. The major difference, however, is the lack of payments to mercenaries. These must have accounted for a very large proportion of south Italian coinage, but very little of Rome's, due to her different military system. The absence of these payments might also partly explain the small scale of Roman coinage compared with that of south Italy or Carthage. Even so it is hard to avoid the impression that Roman coinage was too small for all state expenditure, and that the 'public sector' at Rome was not completely monetarised: military pay, at any rate, was not at first paid in coin, nor were many other payments. At the other end of the spectrum of the use of coinage, one can see that the absence of any substantial bronze coin issues before the First Punic War precludes the use of Roman coinage for the daily needs of retail trade.

The adoption of coinage

In view of this, third-century Rome may be seen as half-way between a society without coinage and one that was fully monetarised. At first money functioned only as a measure of value. Originally, animals had been used for making comparisons of relative values, just as in the Homeric world, where the price of goods was assessed in so many cows, but actually paid in other goods. However, perhaps in the sixth century, property qualifications for the different Roman classes were established on the basis of metal, and in the fifth century bronze by weight replaced animals as the medium of the assessment of fines: actual payments would no doubt have been made in various goods, including metal. At this time, bronze circulated by weight in the form of fragments, aes rude (rough bronze), and of ramo secco bars. In the late fourth and early third centuries the Romans, in their dealings with the Greeks of south Italy, presumably used Greek coins, but as the production of their own coinage increased, the extent to which their society became monetarised also gradually increased. In this, as in so many other respects, the Hannibalic War seems to have played a decisive role, as from that period the quantity of money available in all denominations seems to have greatly increased, and so coinage became able to play a fuller role in the economic activities of the Romans.

We can in this way trace in broad outline the development of money and coin in Rome, but there is still the puzzle of why the Romans decided to start making coins at this precise time. Why did they need them then, when they had not before? Why did they not continue to use the coinage of other states, as happened in other ancient states such as Sparta, and as the Romans did themselves later in Spain, Greece and Asia? What were the special conditions in about 300 BC which prompted them to inaugurate their own coinage?

At first this coinage was small, unintegrated and sporadic; it was not forced on Rome by any commercial or military considerations, indeed it was not necessary for them to make their own coinage at all. It is possible, though perhaps surprising, to see the beginning of coinage at Rome in cultural terms, as the desire to adopt a Greek institution. We know that in the years around 300 BC the Romans received many cultural influences from Greece and the Greek communities in southern Italy; so much so that it became possible to describe Rome as a 'Greek city' at about this time, with the implication of civilisation and contrast with barbarism. A particularly clear instance of the hellenisation of Rome at this period is provided by pottery. The technique of black glaze was adopted from south Italy, and the decoration applied also shows the same influence; for instance,

15

some of the stamps used to impress decoration on Roman pottery copy Syracusan, Tarentine or Heraclean coins.

Similarly, the designs on Roman coinage, the cast bronzes as well as the struck coins, were totally Greek in inspiration. The types as a whole were influenced by the iconography of Alexander the Great, for example, the diadem worn by Hercules (8) or the lion of Alexander's signet ring (7), and there are several precise instances of influence from south Italy: for instance, the pegasus on the Corinthian coins which circulated in Sicily was copied or adapted on all elements of the early Roman coinage. In this and many other examples one can see that the appearance of the coinage is completely Greek in style, but for the Latin inscriptions.

As well as design, the method of manufacture was also Greek: the Romans copied the method of making coins from the Greek colony of Naples, as can be seen from the close similarities of fabric and weight between the very earliest Roman and contemporary Neapolitan coins. Moreover, the institution of coinage itself was Greek, and coins were only rarely produced much beyond the borders of the Greek world. The Roman coinage seems in all these ways to be completely hellenised from its inception, and in this respect forms a close analogy with contemporary pottery. In coinage, as in pottery, Rome imported many Greek ideas, but these did not sweep away the previous non-Greek traditions. Both pottery and coinage produced hybrid forms, mixtures of south Italian and central Italian elements. The aes grave was thus a hybrid between the Greek idea of round coins and the heavy bronze currency of south Italy.

The Romans' desire to make their own coinage, rather than to continue without or to make use of that of another state, can therefore be seen in the same light as the adoption of 'Greek' pottery: both were aspects of the intense hellenisation of Rome at this period. Roman coinage did not result from any economic or military necessity, and could at first fulfil only the most limited functions. It arose, arguably, from the cultural influence of Greece and the Greek cities in southern Italy: the Romans wanted their city to have the civilisation of Greek cities, and saw the production of their own coinage as one important aspect of this process.

PART TWO

Chapter Two

Authority, control and organisation

Authority

In the ancient world it was thought that the authority under which coinage was produced emanated from the sovereign power in any state. A Hellenistic pamphlet (the *Oeconomica*, once attributed to Aristotle)·distinguished between the different sorts of responsibilities proper to an individual, a city, a provincial governor and a king, and included decisions about coinage among the responsibilities of the king (1345*b* 20). This theory can be seen in practice in the letter sent by the Syrian King Antiochus VII (138–129 BC) to his subject the Jewish prince Simon Maccabees: "I permitted you to make your own coins in your own country" (I Maccabees 15.6). In the Roman Republic there is no explicit statement that the authority for coinage was vested in the sovereign power, the people, but it clearly was, since changes to or reforms of the coinage were introduced by legislation passed by the popular assembly, and since the people probably elected the moneyers who were actually responsible for the production of the coinage. As in many other ways, however, the people's theoretical power was in practice overshadowed by that of the senate, which for all effective purposes controlled the annual state budget and the production of coinage.

With the establishment of the empire by Augustus (31 BC–AD 14), however, authority resided in the emperor, and this link between coinage and the emperor's sovereignty was perceived by contemporaries. Alleged coins issued in the name of Tigidius Perennis, the praetorian prefect of Commodus, were regarded as evidence of a plot to seize the throne (Herodian 1.9.7), while, rather startlingly, to carry a coin with the imperial image into a lavatory or a brothel could be regarded as treasonable (Suetonius, *Tiberius* 58). Later, for instance in the fourth century, one of the first acts of the usurper Procopius (AD 365–66) to legitimise his position was to mint gold coins with his name and image (Ammianus 26.7.11). The practical aspect of this imperial sovereignty over coinage is spelled out in the story of how a

17

prophet from the city of Abonouteichos in Asia Minor petitioned the emperor Marcus Aurelius for permission to strike a new coin with the magic snake Glycon on one side and himself on the other with the wreaths of his grandfather the god Asclepius and the harpa of his uncle Perseus (Lucian, *Alexander* 58). This is a rather colourful example of a local dignitary asking the emperor for permission to make coins. Similarly we know from an inscription that a man called Claudius Candidus Julianus visited Rome in 127, on behalf of his city (Hadrianopolis Stratonicea in Asia Minor), to petition the emperor Hadrian on various matters, presumably including coinage since on Hadrianic coins of that city Candidus's name appears with the information that he was 'the petitioner' (in Greek *aitesamenos*). The successful outcome of such petitions is sometimes recorded on coins which declare that they were struck by permission of the emperor. Examples are PERM(issu) CAESARIS AVGVSTI or PERM DIVI AVG at Emerita and Romula in Spain, or PERM IMP at Corinth under Domitian; similarly at Patras in Greece one finds the legend MONETA INPETRATA INDVLGENTIAE AVG or "coin obtained through the indulgence of the emperor".

These examples show that at least in theory the emperors could perceive themselves, and were perceived by others, as being the power which authorised coinage. Yet this is an oversimplification which requires several qualifications. First, cities might also seek permission from provincial governors, be they legates of the emperor in "imperial" provinces (for example PERMISSV SILANI, referring to the legate Silanus, at Berytus in Phoenicia in AD 11–17) or proconsular governors in "senatorial" provinces (for example PERM L VOLVSI PROCOS, referring to the proconsul L. Volusius Saturninus, at a city in Africa in 7–6 BC). Moreover, permission might be asked for the right in perpetuity as at Romula and Italica in Spain where Augustus's permission was also declared on coins of Tiberius (PERM AVG, then PERM DIVI AVG after Augustus's death and deification), or, apparently, on each individual occasion, as on coins traditionally attributed to Clypea in Africa (**71**), which record the permission of three successive proconsular governors:

PERMISSV L APRONI PROCOS III	AD 20/1
PERMIS Q IVN BLAESI PROCOS IT	AD 22/3
PERMIS P CORNELI DOLABELLAE PROCOS	AD 23/4

Another instance of the way in which the authority of the emperor might be delegated to another person or body concerns the notorious letters SC, standing for *Senatus Consulto* or "By decree of the Senate", which appear prominently on virtually all imperial bronze coins, but not on those made of precious metal. The interpretation of these letters has been one of the most vexed questions of modern numismatics. In the nineteenth century it was thought that sc implied a dyarchy between the emperor, who controlled coinage in gold and silver, and the senate, which controlled base metal coinage. In modern times, however, this view has become untenable with the realisation that the separation of the power of the emperor and that of the senate is unreal. There was no sharp division of responsibilities, as was once thought.

New explanations have therefore been offered. One holds that the letters refer to the designs used on the coins: for instance the wreath on sestertii of Augustus (**60**) was one of the honours voted to him by decree of the senate, and hence the letters sc are present on the coins. However, this view is not satisfactory, as there are several cases where sc appears without any appropriate honour on bronze coins (**63**), and where an appropriate honour appears on gold or silver coins, but without sc. A more recent theory sees the decree of the senate as the means with which Augustus introduced new metals for the base metal coinage (brass and copper instead of leaded bronze), and that the prominent use of sc on these coins was to provide some sort of guarantee for the public about these new metals. This view, however, does not account for the absence of sc on the earliest of the new coins (e.g. **59**), or its presence on the coinage of Antioch (**65**), which was not made of these new metals. Probably the most reasonable explanation is that Augustus used a decree or several decrees of the senate (one of his regular methods of introducing reform) to regularise the coinage. On this hypothesis, one of these provided that the moneyer Cn Piso (in 23 BC) should introduce brass and copper coins at the mint of Rome; another that the bronze coinage of Antioch should be reformed, as it was in 5 BC by the imperial legate of Syria, Quinctilius Varus. In both cases, the decree of the senate was the administrative means used to institute the reforms, in an "imperial" province as well as at Rome. In this sense, particularly given Augustus's claim to have restored the Republican constitution (**55**), the authority for the coins derived from the senate. This was, however, no more a real power than when in 44 BC Julius Caesar had a senatorial decree passed authorising the placing of his portrait on the coinage (**45**).

A second, and more important, qualification of the emperor's authority over coinage is the question of how widespread was the practice of asking for and receiving permission to coin. It is sometimes thought that such permission was not actually required, and that its (unnecessary) asking and recording on coins is merely a form of flattery to the emperor or provincial governor. This view, however, is susceptible neither of proof or disproof, and, while we may agree that it seems unlikely that every single issue of coinage sought and received permission, we do know (for example, from the letters of the younger Pliny when he was governor of the province of Bithynia in the early second century) that the Roman authorities were closely involved in even fairly minor decisions by cities. It therefore seems likely that petitioning and receiving permission took place frequently, even if not on every possible occasion.

Control of the coinage

The mint of Rome in the Republic
In the Republic, the Roman state budget was controlled by the senate; the *aerarium* or treasury was under the control of senior annual magistrates, the quaestors, and the coinage was the responsibility of three (increased briefly to four by Julius Caesar) more junior magistrates, the *tresviri auro argento aere flando feriundo*, abbreviated to IIIVIRI AAAFF and meaning "the board of three, responsible for casting and striking gold, silver and bronze". Exactly when this board of three annual magistrates was instituted is not clear: the full title does not appear before imperial times, but IIIVIR is first attested on denarii of Mn Aquilhius in about 71 BC (**29**), and AAAFF in 44 BC. Yet the moneyers certainly existed much earlier; the earliest clear case is the denarii minted by the men who abbreviated their names to Cn Dom, L Coil and Cn Calp. Their coins were made from a shared pool of obverse dies, a good indication that all three were working together and can therefore be regarded as the first definite board of three moneyers, in about 180 BC. It has sometimes been thought that the office was created more than a century earlier, in 289 BC, but this is based on too precise a reading of an antiquarian text of Pomponius. The most likely date seems to be that of the denarius coinage, in 212 BC.

The precise method by which the provision of coinage was controlled under the Republic is not, of course, clear. It seems likely that, while the moneyers – no doubt together with the treasury quaestors – were responsible for the actual running of the mint and the production of coinage, they will not have taken the major decisions. Presumably each year the senate set an annual budget, including a requirement for the provisions of new coin; the quaestors would be authorised to transfer the correct amount of bullion or other stock of metal from the treasury to the mint (which was in the Temple of Juno Moneta on the Capitoline Hill), where the moneyers, perhaps each working for a third of a year (one moneyer states that he PRI FL or 'struck first': **34**) or in conjunction, would arrange for it to be turned into coin. The coins would then presumably be returned to the treasury to be issued when appropriate; we hear for instance of 'stipendium' (military pay) being sent with armies from Rome, for example to Africa with Pompey in 82 BC (Plutarch, *Pompey* 11). From time to time the amount of authorised new coin must have proved inadequate, and moneyers, or indeed other magistrates, were authorised to produce supplementary issues, at least sometimes marked SC or EX SC. A particularly flagrant case is in 58 BC when an enormous special issue (**32**) was authorised under the aedileship of M Scaurus and P Hypsaeus, presumably to pay for the games which they as aediles were responsible for organising. Such was the extravagance of these games that they were later thought to mark a turning point in the moral corruption of Rome (Pliny, *Natural History* 36.24.113).

The actual standards of weight and fineness for the different denominations were fixed by law: examples are the *lex Clodia* of about 100 BC which appears to have reintroduced the silver quinarius with victory designs (**25**), and the *lex Papiria* of about 92 BC, which reintroduced the silver sestertius and reduced the weight standard of the bronze coinage by 50 per cent. Thus the specifications of the coinage were set by law, and the volume of coinage to be produced was probably set by the senate; only the actual organisation of the coinage's production was left to the moneyers. Even so they, or the permanent workers at the mint, depending on the extent to which responsibility was delegated by the moneyers, had enough scope profoundly to affect the physical appearance of the coinage, particularly in terms of the design used.

At the beginning of the denarius coinage (**17–21**), most of the designs used had been centrally chosen, presumably by the senate. This is clear since the numerous mints (one at Rome, two in Sicily, one in Sardinia, one in Lucera, at least one in Spain and others at uncertain locations) set up in the second half of the Hannibalic War to effect the great recoinage of the denarius all used the same design for the same denominations. Variation occurs only on the three extremely rare issues of the half-victoriate, where each of the three mints responsible chose a completely different design. This suggests that fairly detailed instructions were sent out centrally, but they did not foresee the local conditions which might require the production of unusual denominations, such as the half-victoriate. As the designs for these were not specified, the mints were free to choose what they thought appropriate. The design specified for the denarius itself was the head of the goddess Roma on the obverse and the two Dioscuri on horseback on the reverse (**17**); later the reverse was changed to a figure of Victory in a chariot, referring to Rome's final defeat of the Macedonian kingdom in Greece in 168 BC (**22**). This initial standardisation of design lasted for some seventy years, but later Republican denarii are characterised above all by the variety of the designs which were used. At first an increasingly full reference was made to the moneyer's name: punning symbols (e.g. **21**) and monograms gave away to fuller forms of the name (**22**). Towards the end of the second century the moneyers began to replace the traditional designs with individual designs which often had political relevance. The decisive step towards these individual designs (referring in various obscure ways to the moneyer or his family) from the previous public design (referring to the state) came in about 137 BC, with the coins of Ti Veturius (**23**), which were the first to refer to the history of a moneyer's ancestor and which at the same time commented on contemporary politics. From this time on, coin designs often commented on contemporary events or, more usually, advertised the origins and family history of the moneyer himself, for example successes like the conquest of Sicily (**29**), achievements and even, later, the portraits of ancestors or parents. This variety of types began, as has been seen, in the 130s BC, and is probably a consequence of the passing of a law (the *lex Gabinia*) in 139 BC, which enforced secret balloting at Roman elections. The moneyership suddenly became more popular among Roman nobles, since coins provided an opportunity for the self-advertisement which now became necessary to launch a successful political career.

One aspect of this freedom of the moneyer to choose the design concerns the use of control systems, particularly in the first century BC. These were apparently intended to keep track of the production of the coinage and the dies used to strike it. Various different systems were used, and, conveniently for us, these frequently involved the engraving on the dies of various control marks, numbers (**27** reverse), letters, or other small symbols, such as everyday items like shoes or knives. Some control marks (different for each die) are found on the obverse only, some on the reverse only, and some on both sides (both as related and unrelated pairs). For instance, denarii of P Crepusius have a simple numeral (from 1 to 525) on the reverse, and on the obverse some twenty-four symbols, each paired with each of the letters of the Latin alphabet (**27**).

These systems became self-consciously and artificially complex, parallelling the choice of increasingly obscure designs. This tendency seems to be more a part of the studied experimentation in the coinage of the time, rather than representing genuine attempts to improve quality control. Although they were not free to change the weight and fineness of the coinage, the moneyers attempted to use the maximum variation possible within these prescribed limits. The variety of design and control symbols has already been mentioned; the moneyers also experimented with the physical appearance of the flans used for the coinage. On one occasion the moneyer C Licinius Macer (84 BC) decided to make unusually thin and broad coins: sometimes these are up to 24mm in diameter (**26**) rather than the normal 17mm. A more regular form of variation was the use of serration, whereby the flan of the coin was produced to look like a cog-wheel, with notches or serrations all the way round the edge (**30**). This was used first on an isolated issue of denarii in Gaul in 118 BC, but the heyday of its use was the first half of the first century BC. It may have originally been intended as a precaution against plated forgeries (more a theoretical than a real precaution, as hundreds of plated serrate denarii prove), but it was mainly used as an artistic device, as it had been in the Greek world a century before. For instance it might appear on one part of an issue but not the other. During some of this period there seem to have been only two engravers at the mint, and at least on some occasions, for example the coins of C. Hosidius Geta (**30–31**), the dies of one engraver were used on serrate flans, and those of the other on non-serrate flans.

The provinces in the Republic
The denarii from the mint of Rome represent the mainstream of the Republican coinage, but they were not the only Roman coins of this period. Denarii were also minted at temporary provincial mints. Most were signed by Roman governors or generals, such as the denarii produced by the general C Annius in 82–81 BC at Marseille and later in Spain (**28**). Other coinages, not denarii (*see* chapter three), do not normally bear any reference to their authority. On the face of it they are just civic Greek coins, yet occasionally they refer to the Roman proconsul or governor, for instance on coins attributed to Atarneus, civic bronzes of

Bithynia from the 50s BC (**41**), and, most famously, cistophori of Asia from about 58 BC (**42**). Similarly some of the tetradrachms of the new Roman province of Syria in 58 BC bear the monogram of the governor Gabinius (**43**). These instances merely recorded the name of the proconsul, and in one case use the Greek preposition *epi* meaning "under" or "during the time of". It seems likely that these are not just a means of dating the coins, but can be interpreted to imply that they were produced under the control of the provincial governors, somewhat like the Greek coinage under the Roman empire.

This control of coinage by the provincial governor became increasingly important towards the end of the Republic and during the civil wars of the first century, mirroring the decline of the power of the senate and the growth of the power of the warlords of the late Republic, whose position was based on the resources of their ever-increasing provincial commands. This shift in minting authority became particularly clear during times of civil war, since the leaders in the provinces then chose – probably illegally – to produce denarii, no doubt for the reasons of prestige and self-advertisement as well as perhaps responding to the preference of their troops. These denarii followed the traditional pattern and had the usual variety of explicit designs and legends, rather than the more anonymous Greek style of coinage. The first clear instance occurs with Sulla, although his denarii were produced within Italy, but from the beginning of the civil war between Pompey and Caesar in 49 BC, the production of denarii outside Italy by the leaders of the different factions became widespread. The majority of the coinage produced in the thirteen years of civil war after the death of Caesar in 44 BC (e.g. **46**), particularly during the final struggle between Octavian and Antony, was produced outside Rome, and entirely on the "authority" of the leaders.

These issues were sometimes produced by the commanders in conjunction with one of their subordinates; the most frequent of these was the quaestor, who is named on the denarii of C Annius (**28**) or the tetradrachms minted by the praetor Cae . . . in Macedonia in the early first century BC (**40**). Other officers are also mentioned: generals, propraetors, proquaestors, and particularly legates, in one case a *legatus F C* which may be short for "legatus fisci castrensis" or "lieutenant of the military treasury".

The empire

The exact extent of the interest in and control of the coinage by the emperor is not completely clear, and it is a subject to which we will return in chapter four. Here it suffices to say that the emperor might take an interest, as is apparent from the effect that a patron of the arts like Nero (AD 54–68) could have on the artistic quality of the coinage (82), or the reversal in the debasements of the silver coinage which took place after the accession of highly moralistic emperors like Domitian (AD 81–96) or Pertinax (AD 193).

The importance of the emperor as the authority for imperial coinage has already been discussed. It began with the gradual increase in the power of provincial governors: it became *de facto* the prerogative of the leaders in the civil war. With the establishment of civil peace by Octavian (later called Augustus) in 31 BC and his political settlements over the next few years, however, the control of the coinage underwent a change, broadly reflecting the need to combine the power Augustus derived from his victory with the traditional constitutional practices, including that of the coinage.

Apart from the control of provincial civic bronze issues (see above) there were three main elements in the emperor's control over the mainstream of the coinage (the gold, silver and bronze minted mainly at Rome), although the exact relationship between them is not entirely clear. Most important seems to have been the *a rationibus*, one of the most important imperial secretaries, who were the men by whom the emperor controlled the empire. The *a rationibus* was the secretary in charge of finances; his origins may lie in Caesar's appointment of "his own slaves in charge of the mint and state revenues" (Suetonius 76). In the first century this secretaryship, like the others, was held by imperial freedmen; under Claudius (AD 41–54) the *a rationibus* was the notorious Pallas, one of the richest men of the day and extremely influential in contemporary politics. After the reign of Claudius a reaction began to set in against the extravagant position of such imperial freedmen, and so we know less about subsequent holders of the secretaryship. Pallas's successor in AD 55 may have been another freedman (called Phaon), and the next known holder of the position (probably from AD 70 until 82) was the father of a man called Claudius Etruscus. He was originally a freedman, but was raised by Vespasian in 73 or 74 to equestrian rank (the status which required a property qualification of 400,000 sestertii and was second only to senatorial status). After the subsequent reorganisation of the imperial civil service, whereby most senior posts came to be held by equestrians graded by the amount of salary they received (60, 100 or 200,000 sestertii), the *a rationibus* was always an equestrian. The first known holder was L Vibius Lentulus in the reign of Trajan, and from that time the post was the most senior in the imperial administration. In the reigns of Marcus Aurelius and Commodus he was the only one to command a salary of 300,000 sestertii. He was, of course, only the head of a large department, about which we know very little. He was assisted by the *procurator summarum rerum* (a post with a salary of 200,000); both he and the *a rationibus* were assisted by senior freedmen, and we hear briefly in inscriptions of many other officials, such as *tabularii*, 'accountants', *adiutores*, 'junior clerical assistants', and many other slaves and freedmen, about whom we know nothing except that they worked for the department. Freedmen are not, however, recorded from the reign of Septimius Severus (AD 193–211), and their likely absence reflects the increasing militarisation of imperial administration from this time.

We do not know a great deal about the exact responsibilities of the *a rationibus*. According to Pliny (*Epistles* 8.6) he was officially known as 'custos principalium opum" or 'Guardian of the Imperial Wealth', but this gives little idea of the huge range of his responsibilities. The best source for this is a poem written in AD 92 or 93 by Statius, consoling Claudius Etruscus on the death of his father, who had held the position earlier:

"To him alone is entrusted control of the sacred treasure, the wealth acquired from every people and the revenue of the great world. Whatever Spain throws out from her gold mines, whatever glitters on Dalmatian mountains, whatever comes from African harvests, whatever is threshed beside the hot Nile . . . all is entrusted to his control alone. . . . Vigilant and wise is he, and quick to work out how much Roman arms under every sky need, how much the city tribes and temples need, how much the tall aqueducts, the forts by the sea or the widely spread network of roads require; how much gold is to shine on the high ceilings of our master, what weight of metal should be melted in the fire and shaped into the divine features, how much is to ring when stamped in the fire of Italian Moneta" (*Silvae* III.iii.86–105).

Even allowing for exaggeration, the poem indicates a wide responsibility for the income and expenditure of the empire, in terms both of cash and commodities (wheat and precious objects). As well as budgeting for expenditure on the army, public works and roads, he specifically has control over how much metal is to be turned into coin in the mint, 'Italian Moneta'.

Unfortunately it is difficult to see in practice the influence of the individual *a rationibus*; even for the sensational Pallas, there is nothing about the coinage which can be particularly attributed to him. We can, however, say something specific about the father of Claudius Etruscus. He was suddenly banished by the emperor Domitian in 82, shortly after Domitian's accession and just before the reform of the coinage, when Domitian restored the fineness of the silver to an earlier pure standard and raised the quality of the manufacture of the coins. Thus, despite the (according to Statius) unrivalled virtue of the father of Claudius Etruscus, he must have been blamed for the low purity and artistic quality of the coinage in the reigns of Vespasian and Titus, and which, by attracting Domitian's displeasure, led to his banishment.

The actual running of the mint was controlled by another official, the *procurator Monetae*, an equestrian official with a salary of 100,000 sestertii. The earliest known is L Vibius Lentulus, who was procurator either in the reign of Nerva (AD 96–98) or early in the reign of Trajan (AD 98–117), and procurators are recorded occasionally throughout the rest of the period under discussion. The post seems mainly to have been an administrative one, not requiring any particular financial or monetary expertise, as most of the known postholders had military backgrounds and did not tend to go on to more senior financial positions.

The other officials recorded are the *tresviri monetales*, whose existence as annually chosen magistrates was revived by Augustus in about 23 BC (**60–63**), perhaps as part of his revival of the Republican constitution. Under Julius Caesar, in the 40s BC, the moneyership had been one of the minor magistracies grouped together as the 'vigintisexvirate' (board of 26), and when Augustus reduced this body to 20 (the 'vigintivirate'), the moneyership continued to play the same role as one of the minor magistracies, the holding of which was required as a precondition for admission to the senate (*Dio* 54.26.6), and moneyers are recorded in inscriptions down to the middle of the third century. How many moneyers there were each year is not known, although the fact that Augustus restored their title from the Caesarian IIIIVIRI AAAFF to IIIVIRI AAAFF might seem to imply that there were normally only three; yet already late in the reign of Augustus some coins show that four men could hold the office concurrently (**63**). The moneyers were, however, particularly favoured among the vigintivirate, and the offspring of noble families destined for high office (the consulship) could expect to hold it rather than any of the other minor magistracies, the "four responsible for roads", the "ten responsible for courts" and the "three responsible for capital punishment":

office	no. known*	from noble families	from new families	reaching consulship
Moneyer	48	17	1	12+
Roads	3	–	3	–
Courts	14	2	8	4
Capital	7	1	3	–

*in the Julio-Claudian period, 31 BC–AD 68

Yet the moneyership did not, any more than the office of procurator Monetae, seem to have required or conferred any particular financial training – none of the known prefects of the treasury or the military pension fund had previously been a moneyer. It was simply part of a gilded career, and one therefore naturally wonders exactly how much, if any, real control over the coinage was exercised by the moneyers under the empire. On the other hand, under Augustus at least, it seems clear that the moneyers had some say in the designs used on the coinage; not the designs used on the new bronze, which kept to the Republican tradition of an unchanging type, but those on the gold and silver, which for a few years immediately after 19 BC displayed a bewildering variety of types, mostly related to the person or family to the moneyer, rather than the emperor. Yet the Augustan moneyers' coinage, which self-consciously revived the habits of the Republic, is quite untypical of imperial coinage. Even by the end of the reign of Augustus, the moneyers had been deprived of the right to choose designs and put their names on the coinage, just as prominent generals who were not members of the imperial family were deprived of the right to celebrate triumphs. From this time on, the moneyers seem to have had no more than a ceremonial rôle and function. Real decisions were taken by the a rationibus, although it remains possible that the moneyers had some influence over the choice of designs, unless that too was a function of the permanent staff of the mint.

Organisation

According to Livy, writing early in the reign of Augustus, "the temple and workshop of Moneta" were on the Capitoline Hill (ubi aedes et officina Monetae nunc est: 6.20.13). This was presumably the site of the mint of Rome in the Republic as well. By the second century AD a series of inscriptions (dating from 115) reveals from their findspots that the mint had been moved to the Caelian Hill (e.g. *ILS* 1634–5), where it seems to have remained, at least until the late third century (Aurelius Victor, *de Caes.* 35.6).

One of the second-century inscriptions (*ILS* 1634) gives the titles of some of the personnel who worked in the mint, corporately known as '*familia monetalis*'. There was the *optio et exactor auri argenti et aeris*, "the inspector (?) and superintendent of gold, silver and bronze", another *optio*, who like the first was a freedman, 24 *officinatores* "section workers", some of whom were freedmen and some slaves. Another inscription (*ILS* 1635) mentions the same *optio et exactor*, together with some *signatores, suppostores* and *malleatores* ("engravers", "placers" and "hammermen": perhaps the people who cut the dies, placed the blanks between the dies and worked the hammers for striking them). But, apart from the nomenclature they reveal, these inscriptions throw little light on the internal organisation of the mint. A little more can be gleaned from law codes, which show, for instance, that mint workers were capable of stealing dies from the mint (*see* chapter five), but the main source of information about the system of production within the mint is the examination of the coins themselves. We know that by the reign of Philip in the third century AD the mint was organised into six parallel sections which were minting concurrently (though not necessarily in equal quantities) and it has been suggested that each section worked in a cycle, producing coins of different denominations and metals in rotation. The fact that, generally speaking, six different reverse designs seem to have been produced at the same time enables one to read this six section organisation back earlier in the third century, but it is quite uncertain when the system began; before the link between a particular design and a particular section became normal, it is obviously much harder to establish the internal organisation of the mint. In the Republican period, however, a division of the mint's operation into the two sections has been suggested, both on the basis of the apparent use of two different engravers for the dies and on the pattern of control marks used. Its divisions in the early empire are, however, unclear.

Of other mints we know even less, not even their precise location. Between 46 and 44 BC, Julius Caesar set up a separate mint for coining the gold he had taken from Gaul and from the Roman treasury; the individual style of the coins (**44**) and the fact that one of the officials who signed its products was a Prefect of the City reveal that it had its own engravers and was situated in Rome, but no more. We are almost equally in the dark about the great mint which Augustus established at Lyon in about 15 BC as the principal gold and silver mint for the whole empire. There are two inscriptions which tell us little, except that it was guarded by an urban cohort, and had a slave called Nobilis who was *aeq(uator) monet(ae)* or 'Mint checker'(?) in the reign of Tiberius (*CIL* 13.1499 and 1820). Apart from these, however, we would probably never even have suspected that it was situated at Lyon, had not Strabo remarked that "the emperors struck coins of gold and silver there" (4.3.2). For its subsequent history, we are entirely dependent on the coins themselves, but they are frustratingly unhelpful. We are not even sure when the gold and silver mint was returned to Rome, where it must have been in Otho's reign (AD 69) and where it subsequently remained. Dates in 38, 54, 64 and 68 have all been suggested, with greater or lesser plausibility, but there is no obvious break in the coinage: whenever it was moved it must have been moved in its entirety, as the sequence of coins shows no very significant stylistic or technical break.

Our ignorance of mints in the provinces and their organisation is almost complete, as there is no independent evidence and the coins themselves rarely reveal anything. Yet over the last few years it has increasingly become clear that these mints were not necessarily always independent operations, but that they could co-operate and even be centrally directed. The best evidence for central direction has come from the study of the fineness of the silver coins minted in the provinces, since it has been shown that on the rare occasions (like the reign of Domitian) when the trend towards the greater debasements of the denarius was reversed at Rome, an analogous improvement in silver fineness took place in the silver minted in the provinces, for example in Cappadocia. Similarly one can see how resources could be switched from one mint to another. For example, Neronian silver was transferred from Cappadocia to Syria with the changing position of the general Corbulo; or, again, the minting of silver was moved from Syria to Alexandria in 219.

Co-operation between mints took place at a lower, more *ad hoc* level, but was fairly widespread, at least from the end of the first century AD. One of the most interesting developments of recent numismatics is the growing awareness that coins were not necessarily minted where they appear to have been. A very clear case concerns some coins of Severus Alexander (AD 222–235) which were minted only for circulation in Egypt, which had its own closed currency system. Some of these coins were minted locally at Alexandria (**107**), but others, superficially exactly similar (**108**, compare **109** from Rome), were minted at Rome and then sent out to Egypt. Other fairly clear cases of this phenomenon concern Syrian coins of Philip (AD 244–49), some of which were minted in Antioch and some in Rome, and bronzes of Vespasian and Trajan minted for circulation in Cyprus, all of which seem to have been minted in Rome. We should not, however, see the phenomenon simply in terms of the huge mint at Rome helping out on rare occasions, since such examples of inter-mint co-operation seem reasonably frequent and do not necessarily involve Rome. Some Syrian coins of Trajan seem to have been minted at Alexandria, which may also have been the mint of some of the Syrian silver of Domitian. Similarly some 'Arabian' drachms of Trajan may have been minted at Antioch, which may also have produced silver for Crete. All these examples are based on the observation that the coins in question have a style unlike the normal style of their local mints, and characteristic of another mint. This suggests at least that the dies were engraved at the other mints, and one can then examine the physical properties of the coins to see whether it seems likely that the coins as well as the dies were made at the other mint: for instance, if they have a metallic composition different from the one and more like the other. Exactly how widespread was this co-operation between mints is hard to define. There seems to have been no regular system as such; rather the pattern seems to be that a large mint might be asked to help out when a smaller local need arose, on an irregular, if relatively frequent, basis.

Something of the same is true of the system of production of the civic coins minted in the provinces, although this did develop in a much more systematic way. At the beginning of the imperial period, the existence of extremely similar portraits of an emperor or empress on the coins of neighbouring cities allows one to surmise that they were probably minted from dies engraved by the same (itinerant) die engraver. Examples of this phenomenon can be found in Asia Minor for Tiberius or Agrippina II, or in Crete for Gaius. From later in the first century AD, however, one also finds the same die used for issues of different cities, on a fairly piecemeal basis, and it looks as if the itinerant engraver may well have begun to carry the die around with him from city to city. From the end of the second century, however, these instances of die-links between cities become much more frequent, indeed so frequent that they are the norm rather than the exception. These links, which are not only common but also occur between cities far distant from each other (e.g. coins of Philip, AD 244–49, from Carallia in Cilicia and Blaundus in Asia:

112–13), have prompted the suggestion that the coins of these different cities were actually minted at some independent centre or centres, perhaps twelve for the whole of the province of Asia. This would, of course, have made the coin-making process simpler and safer, as a city would need only to place a contract for coinage to one of these 'workshops', rather than having to provide coin-making machinery and to acquire the necessary dies and bullion.

This system of 'workshops' seem to have begun in north-west Asia Minor in about AD 175, and to have spread fairly slowly from there across Asia (and partly into Syria), becoming the normal method of production for the civic issues there until their cessation in about AD 260. The organisation behind this system is somewhat disputed. One possibility is that it was all privately organised on an entrepreneurial basis, making savings for the cities and profits for the workshops. On the other hand, it has been pointed out that the volatility of production of civic bronzes (*see* chapter 3) would have made the workshop system less attractive as an economic proposition, as there would have been substantial periods without work. An opposing view, therefore, sees the system as being organised by the Roman authorities to ensure the maintenance of an adequate production of bronze coinage, when this showed signs in the late second century of becoming inadequate. This view perhaps gains some support from the consideration that the idea of the 'workshop' probably originated in the way that the mint at Rome made local issues from the late first century onwards: the workshops could be more localised and systematic versions of the same thing.

The overriding impression of the organisation of mints and minting throughout the empire is that it was not based on any clearly preconceived plan or system. Rather, the organisation of the collection of different mints grew up and developed from the situations that the Romans inherited as their empire expanded. It was entirely typical of Roman administration to leave an existing system well alone, and to intervene only in response to specific needs or problems. As will be seen in the next chapter, this attitude explains the surprising diversity of the coinage used in their world.

Chapter Three

Monetary history

The denarius coinage during the Republic

The history of the coinage from its inception in about 300 BC to its collapse in the Hannibalic War (218–201 BC) has already been described. After the collapse, a complete change came over the coinage of the Roman world. Firstly, all earlier coinages were demonetised, that is to say, withdrawn from circulation and melted down. This demonetisation applied not just to the earlier Roman coins, but to virtually all other coins circulating in Italy and Sicily. From then on, only Roman coins were used, as the following table of finds makes clear:

3rd century finds	Roman	non-Roman
River Liri	6	37
Valle d'Ansanto	36	76
Ordona	–	10
Cosa	5	20
2nd century finds		
River Liri	453	8
Ordona	38	–
Cosa	247	8
Minturnae	59	–

Secondly, most of these earlier coins were recoined into Roman silver and bronze coins of the new denarius system, and, to do this, mints were established throughout Italy, Sicily, Sardinia and even Spain. It is not exactly clear why Rome adopted this aggressive new policy of ensuring that all monetary transactions were dominated by Roman coins and thus interposing the authority of the Roman state in all the economic activities of her subject peoples. It was, however, presumably made possible by the Roman victories in Sicily, which would have provided the much-needed bullion (acquired as the spoils of war) that was required for a new Roman coinage after the collapse of the previous one. Yet the desire to replace other non-Roman

coinages with their own did not in itself require the availability of
fresh supplies of bullion, since much of this would have been
provided by the demonetised coins. Another explanation is
therefore needed. Perhaps military successes had given a new
self-confidence to the Romans; if so the change in the currency of
the Roman world could perhaps be seen as a sign that the
Romans sensed victory after years of mauling at the hands of
Hannibal.

The date of this recoinage, which was effected by the
introduction of the denarius (17), used to be one of the most
contentious points in Roman numismatics, but over the last
twenty years or so enough new evidence has come to light,
especially from Sicily, to show beyond reasonable doubt that the
new coinage began in 212 or 211 BC. There are many
considerations in favour of this date, of which only the most
important can be mentioned here. First of all, Sicilian hoards,
such as those from Syracuse and Enna, show that the coinage of
quadrigati (15) was still current in about 215 BC. Secondly, the
earliest denarii (and only the earliest) have been found during the
modern excavations at the site of the Sicilian town of Morgantina,
which according to Livy was destroyed in 211 BC. This suggests
that the coinage had only just begun by this date. Thirdly, two
Carthaginian coins from Sicily have been found to be struck over
early Roman coins of the denarius system: the Carthaginian coins
must have been minted before 210, when the Carthaginians were
driven out of Sicily, so the Roman coins, a denarius and a
victoriate, must have also been minted by then. These, and other
supporting considerations, make it certain that the denarius was
introduced in the middle years of the Hannibalic War: the exact
date is of course open to argument, but 212 seems the most
likely.

The constituent parts of this new denarius coinage were
related to each other in terms of the intrinsic value of their metal
content, although the weight standard of the bronze rapidly fell
off, and the coins became fiduciary or token coins. The coins
were all marked with their values in asses, or parts of the as:

silver		*bronze*		
denarius (17) X	10 asses	as (20)	I	
quinarius (18) V	5 asses	semis	S	half as
sestertius (19) IIS	2½ asses	triens	. . . .	quarter as
		quadrans	. . .	third as
		sextans (24)	. .	sixth as
		uncia	.	twelfth as

The half and quarter of the denarius, i.e. the quinarius and the sestertius (18 and 19), played a relatively minor role as they were struck only rarely, either in times of financial stress in the Hannibalic (218–201 BC), Social (91–88 BC) and Civil (49–44 BC) Wars, or, in the case of the quinarius, in connection with the founding of colonies in Gaul (25). In the latter case the context provides the specific reason, since coins of quinarius weight were the preferred silver denomination in Gaul and widely produced there. In the former case the lower silver purity of quinarii and presumably sestertii may provide the reason, although this explanation does not hold good for the quinarii and sestertii of the Hannibalic War, which apparently have the same purity as contemporary denarii. In this case the explanation may be historical. Rome had previously, if intermittently, produced smaller denominations in silver – the half piece, a twelfth (equivalent to a Greek obol) and perhaps a sixth (a diobol). The quinarius continued the tradition of half pieces; the sestertius was, by weight, equivalent to the south Italian diobol, a denomination which had been produced abundantly in the third century, and it briefly took its place in circulation, as one can see, for instance, from the finds at Rossano near Vaglio (Potenza) which produced fifty-nine south Italian diobols and four Roman sestertii.

In addition to the denarius, quinarius and sestertius, the Romans also produced another silver coin, the victoriate (20), named after the figure of the goddess Victory, crowning a trophy, on the back. The exact rôle of this coin has always been somewhat obscure; although it was minted contemporaneously with denarii (as the use of many shared moneyers' symbols proves), it lacks a value mark and was not normally hoarded together with denarii. However, recent metal analyses have helped to clarify its rôle. These analyses have shown that, whereas the denarius was made of more or less pure silver, the victoriate was made of only 80% silver (the remaining 20% being copper); thus in composition it resembled the earlier quadrigati of the same reduced fineness, which it presumably in some sense replaced. This difference in fineness also explains why victoriates were not hoarded with denarii, even though hoards of either denarii or victoriates are found throughout the same areas in Italy. Presumably it was well known that the victoriate was made of inferior metal, so hoarders took care not to hoard it with pure silver. Initially it was minted in very large quantities, presumably because Roman finances were still hard pressed by the costs of the war and it was in Roman interests to make as many payments in debased silver as possible: until about 170 BC it accounted for the majority of Roman silver in circulation. Only after the defeat of Macedonia in 168 BC, which produced a windfall of 75 million denarii of spoil, did the Roman treasury become solvent: the paying of tribute by Roman citizens was suspended and at the same time the production of the debased silver victoriate was ended. The purer denarius thereafter prevailed.

The bulk of the coinage produced by Rome in the first half of the second century was, however, in bronze, and huge numbers, of asses in particular (21), all with the same designs of a head of Janus on the front and a prow of a ship on the back, were minted down to the middle of the century. The huge scale of minting made the bronze asses relatively common compared to the denarius, and perhaps as a result of this the denarius was in 141 BC re-tariffed at 16 (22, with the value mark XVI) rather than 10 asses, which thereafter remained in force for some 350 years. Second-century bronzes continued to circulate for many years and provided most of the bronze currency in circulation during the rest of the Republic and even into the empire, since very little bronze was minted after 150 BC. At this date the production of silver took off, and the switch from bronze to silver has been associated with a change in the medium of military pay from bronze coins to silver coins. Smaller quantities of bronze, especially of lower denominations than the as, were minted until the end of the century, e.g. 24, a late second-century sextans. There was then a gap until about 92 BC when the *lex Papiria de aeris pondere* reduced the standard of the as to half a Roman ounce, and such coins were minted (the majority made of pure copper rather than bronze) for a few years, sometimes with experimental and varied designs. The lower weight standard and new designs were, however, abandoned by Sulla in 82 BC. At about the same time the lightweight asses were obviously demonetised since, unlike the earlier second-century asses, they are not found in later hoards. After 80 BC no further issues of bronze were made at the mint of Rome until the reign of Augustus, although during the civil wars issues of bronze were made elsewhere in Italy: by Caesar in north Italy in 45 BC, and by Octavian, perhaps in north Italy, in about 38 BC (48), probably in response to the contemporary issues of Sextus Pompey in Sicily and Spain (47). The absence of any substantial production of bronze coinage in the first century BC seems to have contributed to a shortage of small change. This shortage of an adequate supply of bronze coin was the first of several during the Roman period (other notable instances occurring during the reign of

Claudius and in the late empire), all of which provoked a variety of privately made forgeries or imitations (49 is an imitation of 48, 75 of 74), just as a similar shortage in late eighteenth-century England was met by the so-called "medley halfpence", which were privately produced coins loosely based on contemporary halfpennies and farthings. These imitations were widely used, even by official bodies like the army, to judge from their discovery today on the sites of Roman camps, and it is sometimes thought that some of them at least may have been produced by the military authorities.

Provincial silver

Unlike the bronze, however, the silver denarius was produced in very large quantities all through the Republic, particularly during periods of war, such as the Social War with the Italian allies in 91–89 BC or the civil wars between 49 and 31 BC. The Republican denarius, minted mainly at Rome, was, however, only one of the silver coinages produced in the Roman world. Extensive silver coinages were produced also in Spain (36) and in Gaul, both Cisalpine, i.e. northern Italy, and Transalpine (e.g. 38). These coins circulated alongside "Roman" silver. The silver also continued to be minted further east, in Greece, Asia Minor and Syria, after these areas were conquered by Rome and, at least at first, without any accompanying Roman silver. Silver currency of the Roman world in the late Republic then varied widely. In central and southern Italy and in Sicily, from the time of the Hannibalic War, the Roman denarius had a monopoly, as it did in Africa (Tunisia) after its annexation in 146 BC, when all earlier Carthaginian gold and silver coin was demonetised and replaced by denarii, as had happened sixty-five years before in Italy and Sicily. In Spain and Gaul, however, Roman silver circulated alongside locally produced silver, while east of the Adriatic Roman silver did not at first circulate at all. Denarii appeared systematically in central Greece only from the time of Sulla, a century after the start of Roman involvement in the area and fifty years after its annexation. Further east, Roman denarii penetrated Asia Minor, perhaps only from the time of the civil wars of the late first century BC (some one hundred years after annexation), and in Syria probably only from the time of Augustus (some fifty years after annexation). In Greece, denarii came to form a monopoly of circulation; this happened only much later in Asia and never in Syria, where they coexisted with locally produced silver tetradrachms until the middle of the third century (*see* Fig. 3.1 showing the spread of the denarius).

Until such time as the denarius played a major role in the currency of a given area, all state payments (whether income or expenditure) would have had to be made in the local currency, as nothing else was available. As a result there is a problem of interpretation with this locally produced silver (and indeed the local bronze), inasmuch as we have to try and decide the extent to which these coinages were minted by local authorities to meet their own fiscal needs or on instruction or contract from the Roman authorities to meet their needs. There is no way of telling from the designs used on the coins themselves, as these tend to repeat the traditional design used by the different cities on their coins before the advent of Roman rule. One can, however, make a functional distinction, since, at one end of the spectrum, a tiny local issue was in all likelihood minted for some local need, whereas a huge one, e.g. from Roman Antioch, was probably minted in response to Roman needs. Needless to say this distinction is far easier to make in theory than in practice, and most cases fall somewhere between these extremes. Nor should we exclude the possibility of a changing function: for instance the coinage of Ephesus can be regarded as shifting in emphasis from local to Roman.

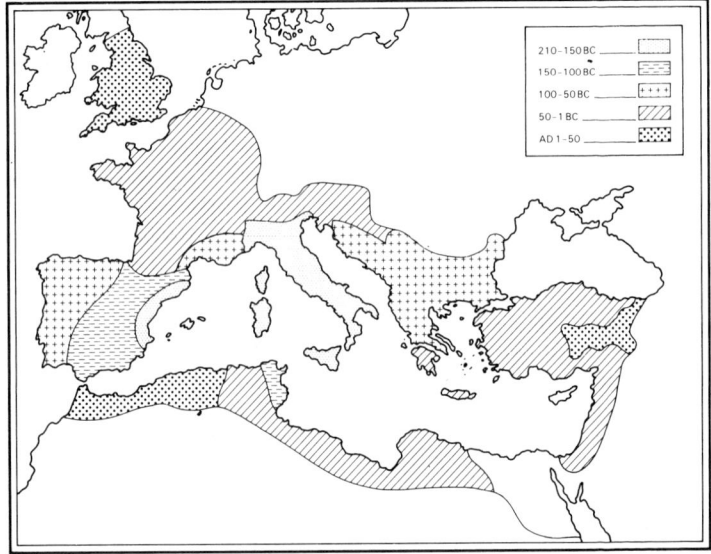

FIG. 3.1 *The Spread of the Denarius*

These local coinages vary widely in their nature; as will be seen from the following short survey, their only common theme is that they illustrate how adaptable the Romans were to different local situations.

Spain

In Spain there were two main local silver issues which seem to have been used by the Romans to a greater or a lesser degree. During the Hannibalic War and immediately thereafter they used imitations of drachms of the town of Emporion (perhaps the "Oscense argentum" mentioned by Livy in 195, 194 and 180 BC), and the number of dies used suggests that these were made in as large a quantity as the silver coined in Spain by Rome's adversaries, the Carthaginians: both coinages, however, were demonetised not long after the war. Some Roman silver was also made in Spain, but these were only tiny issues of victoriates, and there are very few hoards of silver; one imagines that the currency of Spain in the early second century was basically bronze. Hoards of large numbers of Roman denarii are only common from the late second century, when they are often hoarded with the so-called 'Iberian denarii' (**36**). Iberian denarii were similar in shape and weight to Roman denarii, but, as their legends in Celtiberian script show, they were minted at more than fifteen different places (**36** is from Osca). All had the same general design of a bearded male head on the front and, usually, a horseman on the back. The date at which they were first minted is a matter of some dispute, suggested dates ranging from the very early to the quite late second century, and their production appears to have continued until the time of the war against Sertorius in about 70 BC. The places of minting were all in the northern part of Spain, and the pattern of hoarding shows a differential distribution of hoards of just Roman denarii, mixed Roman and Iberian denarii, and just Iberian denarii. In the south, the mixed hoards prevail, whereas further north one tends to find just Roman denarii nearer the coast and just Iberian denarii further inland. Perhaps the most likely explanation for their production and distribution is that they were minted in response to military requirements on the spot, though whether this would include the payment of Roman soldiers as opposed to Spanish auxiliaries in the Roman army is currently disputed. Indeed, other more local functions have also been suggested; yet the hand of the Romans can clearly be seen in the choice of a common design for all mints.

Gaul

The picture of local silver in Gaul is less clear-cut, as Gallic coins present a rather bewildering variety of issues and types, whose chronology and hence historical interpretation is rather unclear. In Cisalpine Gaul, that is to say, the area south of the Alps and north of the river Po, a Celtic and Ligurian coinage of imitations of drachms of Marseille (Massalia) continued to be used from the end of the third century until the late second century, sometimes together with Roman coins. The general similarity of date and hoarding pattern with that of the Iberian denarii suggests a common function. Further north, when Roman involvement north of the Alps began in 125 BC, they at first encountered the silver coinage of Marseille (**38**), which, together with the so-called *monnaie à la croix* from the south-west, remained the main silver currency of southern Gaul until the middle of the first century. In the first century large quantities of other native silver was produced by various tribal communities, like the Aedui or the Sequani, for instance, mostly on the weight standard of the Roman quinarius (**25**). Roman coins, particularly quinarii, started to arrive in the first century, but, despite the presence of a large number of Roman businessmen in the area, Roman coins did not circulate in any quantity before the time of Caesar in the 50s BC.

Greece

Although these local coinages continued to circulate for some time, they were gradually replaced by the denarius, which in the Roman west became virtually the sole silver coin from the reign of Augustus: when Britain was invaded in AD 43, for instance, the local coinages were suppressed and replaced by the denarius in the areas newly annexed. In the eastern half of the empire, however, the denarius did not make much of an appearance before that time, except in Greece. Greece was annexed in 146 BC, the same year as Africa, yet the monetary contrast between the two areas could not be clearer. In Africa the denarius immediately replaced all earlier Carthaginian precious metal coinages; in Greece it did not appear in substantial quantities for another fifty years, a hundred years in the case of the Peloponnese, and most Greek coinages continued unaltered by the Roman conquest. Indeed, from the appearance of the coins alone, such as the coinage of Athens (**39**), one would never have suspected such a profound change in the regime. Only very rarely do coins explicitly acknowledge their Roman origin, for example the tetradrachms produced in Macedonia and signed by a Roman praetor called Cae. . and a quaestor called Aesillas (**40**).

In the absence of Roman coins it is clear that the Romans must have used "Greek" coinages such as those of Athens or Thasos for their own needs at least until the time of Sulla. After that, locally minted silver starts to peter out, although there seems to have been something of a revival in some areas (e.g. the Thessalian League), prompted by the civil wars. The need for cash engendered by these wars, and the necessity to buy the loyalty of the troops, also prompted the leaders of the different factions, for example Brutus (**46**), to mint denarii of the Roman type in Greece, and indeed in Asia. These new denarii of the civil wars effectively replaced the main silver coinages like those of Athens or the Thessalian League – it is possible that they were made out of melted down Greek silver – and from that time on the denarius had a monopoly of the silver currency of Greece.

Asia
When the kingdom of Pergamum (the western part of modern Turkey) was bequeathed by its king Attalus to Rome in 133 BC and subsequently created the Roman province of Asia, the Romans inherited the coinage system of the Pergamene kings. In the mid second century the Pergamene kings had followed the example of the Egyptian kings a century earlier and established their kingdom as a closed currency area, using a currency (the cistophorus) which was of a lower intrinsic value than the coins that circulated in surrounding areas and enforcing its use as the sole silver currency; consequently cistophori did not leave Asia, since outside they were relatively worthless, and foreign silver was not accepted in the kingdom. The Romans maintained this system and indeed the production of cistophori remained unaltered from 133 until 67 BC. During this period the fact that the coinage continued steadily despite changes in the control of the different mints during the Mithradatic Wars suggests that the coinage still had a substantially non-Roman character, although it must obviously have been used by the Romans, as can be seen from the greater level of minting (and an appreciable debasement of the silver purity) during the same Mithradatic wars. In 67 the coinage was interrupted and did not resume until 58 (there is a similar gap in Syria), and this break has been connected with Pompey's enormous commands in the East and his control of its revenues. When the coinage resumed from 58 till 49, it had become more Romanised in design with the name of the Roman governors, for example (**42**) of C Fabius, being added to the traditional design. There are also some rare coins of the famous Cicero. In the 30s earlier issues seem to have been demonetised,

and minting then took place again with two very large issues made by Mark Antony in his struggle against Octavian (**50**). The designs were now dominated by the portrait of Antony. After Octavian's victory he (as Augustus) produced substantial issues from 28 until 18 BC, using no element of the traditional designs. Cistophori had become completely Roman (**57**). Thereafter the minting of cistophori became more occasional; there were small issues under Claudius and in the Flavian period, and a large recoinage of earlier pieces by Hadrian (**93**), perhaps in connection with his tour of the province. The last issue of cistophori was a small issue for the emperor Septimius Severus (AD 193–211). In Asia, as in Greece, denarii of the Roman type were minted early during the civil wars of the late Republic, early in the reigns of Augustus and Vespasian and perhaps also in the reign of Hadrian. It is clear that from the late Republic onwards, although the minting of denarii in Asia was always on a restricted scale, the two sorts of coin coexisted in the province. Large numbers of denarii were imported to form the basis of the imperial silver currency, as we can see from coin finds.

Syria
Other small issues of local silver continued to be minted in the East down to imperial times at places like Aphrodisias, Rhodes and Chios, but rapidly became insignificant in size or died out. Further east, in Syria, a pattern like that of Asia was repeated. Local civic silver had revived in the area in about 100 BC in the wake of the crumbling power of the Seleucid kings; such coinage survived the establishment of the Roman province in 63 BC, and some (e.g. Laodicea) played an important role in the civil wars, but again they tended to peter out with the advent of the empire. The last, purely civic, silver issues of Laodicea date from 17/16 BC, although there were small issues, for example of Augustus and Nero with imperial heads, while Sidon produced its last issue of tetradrachms in 30/29 BC; small issues of half pieces were made in 6/5 BC, AD18/19 and AD 43/4, when the coinage ceased. As in Asia, however, the Romans took over as their principal coinage in the area the previous major royal coinage, in this case the silver tetradrachms minted by the Seleucid kings at Antioch. For the first five years of the new province there seems to have been no coinage, but the arrival of the governor Aulus Gabinius in 58 (the same year that the striking of cistophori was resumed) saw the reorganisation of the tax and financial system of the province. These reforms included the inauguration of a coinage of rather debased silver tetradrachms, minted by the Roman authorities

posthumously in the name of Philip Philadelphus, one of the last Seleucid kings. These Roman coins copied his coins closely, and only added, at first, a monogram of the governor's name (43), or, from the 40s BC, a date. Production continued until the 30s BC, when it was interrupted by the famous tetradrachms of Cleopatra and Antony (51), but resumed after Antony's defeat and continued for the first fifteen years or so of Augustus's reign.

Unlike Asia, Syria seems to have seen little production of denarii during the civil wars. There are only rare possibilities like the denarii of Antony and Cleopatra in view of their similarity to the tetradrachms. The plentiful circulation of denarii there seems to have begun only after the establishment of the empire, even though there is no real evidence for the exact date. To judge from the Bible, denarii clearly played an important role by the reign of Tiberius, but they never supplanted or even dominated the locally produced silver coinage. There were two principal silver coinages in the area during the early empire. These were the tetradrachms of Antioch, which were reformed in 5 BC and thereafter always bore the head of the reigning emperor, and a large coinage of silver shekels which was minted with the name of the city of Tyre, for example (77) of AD 51, although it has been suggested that they were in fact struck in Jerusalem to enable the Jews to pay their annual Jewish tax to the Temple there, as the Tyrian shekels were made of pure silver, whereas the tetradrachms were of debased silver, whose use broke the canons of Jewish belief. In AD 60, however, the Tyrian coinage was absorbed by the Antiochene, and from then the tetradrachms' fineness improved and they bore the shekel's eagle as their reverse design, for example, (80) of Nero. The tetradrachms were then known as "silver of good Tyrian stamp" (*argyrion kalou Tyriou kommatos*), and large numbers were minted during the immediately ensuing years for the campaigns of Corbulo. Thereafter, during the Jewish revolt (AD 66–70) and the civil war of 68–69, a number of branch mints were established in Syria, both for the production of tetradrachms and denarii, whose minting at Antioch is explicitly attested by Tacitus (*Histories* II.82). Thereafter the number of Syrian mints and extent of production was reduced. Although substantial issues were minted under Trajan (98–117), issues during the rest of the second century were small and sporadic. The civil wars of the years following the death of Commodus (AD 192), however, again saw the production of denarii in Syria, and ten years later the production of tetradrachms from a number of Syrian mints resumed, presumably in connection with the wars against the

Persians. Large-scale production continued on and off for some fifty years until the reign of Trebonianus Gallus (AD 251–53), the date which marked the approximate end of the denarius coinage. Thus for the whole of the period, locally produced silver played an important part alongside Roman silver in the province of Syria.

The existence of two different sorts of coinage, each with completely different origins, one Roman and one local or "foreign" (*peregrinus nummus*, as coins like the tetradrachm could still be called in the second century: Maecianus 45), in areas like Asia and Syria raises the question of how the two elements coexisted, both in terms of denominations and functions. There is very little evidence to clarify the function of the two different sorts of coin. It is, however, very noticeable that the production of denarii seems to start up in unfamiliar areas like Asia and Syria during times of civil war, be they the wars of the late Republic, of AD 68–69 or after 193, whereas the production of local silver, in Syria at any rate (or in Cappadocia: *see* below), seems more linked to periods of external warfare, for instance against the Persians. One naturally suspects from this that the different sorts of coin had different rôles. Perhaps, for instance, local silver was required in dealings with provincials to purchase military equipment or food, but denarii were required in official Roman payments (such as payments to soldiers). Moreover, the story of Jesus and the "tribute penny" suggests that Roman taxes had to be paid in Roman silver. Perhaps it is no accident that the arrival of denarii in Syria coincided with the first census there, which was held by the governor Quirinius in AD 6 and which formed the basis of the imperial taxation system of the area.

Cappadocia and Egypt
Two other areas produced major silver coinages in the imperial period, Caesarea in Cappadocia and Alexandria in Egypt. Cappadocia, roughly speaking the eastern end of Asia Minor, became part of the Roman empire on the death in AD 17 of its last king, the pro-Roman Archelaus. The royal mint at the capital Caesarea was also taken over by the Romans on a substantial though irregular basis. The first issues were made late in the reign of Tiberius (68). Some are dated to AD 33–34, and they may have been made in preparation for the campaign of L. Vitellius against the Parthians. A connection with eastern wars is the possible explanation for many of the larger issues from Caesarea, under Nero for the campaigns of Corbulo, under Trajan for his

long Parthian war and particularly in the reign of Marcus
Aurelius (AD 161–80) for the Parthian war fought by his
co-emperor Lucius Verus. Curiously the coins sometimes have
Greek inscriptions and sometimes Latin, and sometimes different languages on different sides of the same coin; these
differences seem to be of no great significance, despite the
attitude of numismatists. At first, issues were made only of the
drachm, the denomination inherited from Archelaus. Already in
the first century, however, its double, the didrachm, was added,
and in the late second century, its triple, the tridrachm, which
continued to be minted until the last issues of Caesarea which
were minted by Gordian III (AD 238–44), again to pay for his
Persian War (**110**). Why the mint was not used after that date is
not clear; perhaps a conscious decision was taken to concentrate
eastern silver minting at Antioch.

The last main area to be discussed is Egypt. As in Cappadocia,
the Romans took over the country and its coinage system
together from its last monarch, in this case from the famous
Cleopatra in 30 BC. Although the Egyptian bronze coinage
minted at Alexandria was reformed in some way under Augustus,
the earlier Egyptian silver currency was taken over by the
Romans and continued to circulate until at least the reign of
Tiberius, to judge from the single surviving hoard, or possibly
until Nero, to judge from references in papyri to "Ptolemaic
silver", which continue until AD 64. Egypt had been the first
Hellenistic kingdom to establish itself as a closed currency area.
In practice this meant that only Egyptian coins circulated within
its boundaries, and that they did not travel outside in any
significant quantity. This was a system which the Romans took
over, as in Asia Minor, and they produced their own silver coins
there from AD 19, in the reign of Tiberius (**69**). Unlike their
practice in Asia, however, they ensured that the system was
maintained for some three hundred years. The minting and
circulation of Egypt's own silver continued from Tiberius to
Diocletian (**130**), and only ended with the reforms of Diocletian
in about AD 296. Consequently imperial Egypt had a currency
system that was unique in the empire: not only did it use its own
coins, which had an artificially high exchange rate compared with
the denarius, but exclusively so, since denarii simply played no
part at all in the currency. In view of the contrast with other
areas, the reason for this is somewhat mysterious. The fact that
the Egyptian kings had made everyone using coins in Egypt
change them into Egyptian coins seems at least partly to have
stemmed from the profit motive, as traders coming to Egypt

would have had to pay a commission on the exchange, and this would have gone to the royal treasury. It may be that this was also the motive of the Roman emperors, particularly in view of the special relationship which existed between Egypt and the emperors, who seem to have regarded it as almost private property.

Roman and local denominations

Thus in some areas of the Roman world the denarius was the only silver coin, having at some stage or other replaced local silver. Elsewhere it circulated alongside local currency, to a greater or lesser degree; while in Egypt it played no part at all. Different solutions were found to the problems of reconciling Roman and pre-existing local systems of accounting and denominations. In some places local systems seem to have died out or been replaced by Roman intervention: for instance an inscription from Thessaly in northern Greece refers to a *diorthoma*, a directive of Augustus replacing reckoning in obols with reckoning in denarii. In other areas local denominations survived, although we do not know exactly how they fitted into the Roman system. In Syria, for instance, the earlier Seleucid system of denominations survived into the imperial period. Exactly when Roman denominations arrived there is not clear. It may have been in the Augustan period, with the reform of the Antiochene coinage in 5 BC or the arrival of the denarius, or early in the reign of Tiberius when Germanicus – further east, at Palmyra – stated that all customs assessments had to be reckoned "in the Italian as", i.e. in Roman denominations. At about the same time the Bible illustrates that, despite the addition of some extra terms like the 'lepton' or widow's "mite", the Roman system of denominations was in general use, and one finds the interesting countermark κο β = "2 quadrantes" on Neronian coins of Caesarea in Samaria. But the Antiochene coinage of Nero (AD 54–68) shows that both systems still existed, since some rare silver coins bear the explanatory inscription *drachme* or *didrachmon* in Greek, while some small bronzes are labelled with the Greek word *chalkous*, the drachm, the didrachm and the chalkous being the earlier Seleucid silver and bronze denominations. The drachma in late Republican and early imperial times periodically changed from ¾ to 1 denarius, in parallel with the changes to the silver fineness of the coins, but from the standardisation of the Syrian silver in AD 60 it seems to have been equivalent to the denarius. This was also the case at Caesarea, where some unusual coins of Nero (**81**) have the label

AC IT KΔ = "24 Italian asses", implying that the normal denomination, the drachma, was equivalent to a denarius.

Elsewhere, however, we can get a more detailed picture of the interrelation of the denarius and the local system. For instance at Tauromenium in Sicily, in the first century BC, the local system of reckoning in one talent of 120 litrae was accommodated to that of the denarius by making an equation between 3 denarii and one talent, or 1 denarius and 40 litrae. This may, however, have been purely for accounting purposes, as there is nothing to suggest that any real coins were still tariffed in litrae. In Asia, however, different denominations also existed as actual coins. The denarius is probably first attested as a value mark on some coins of Aphrodisias of late Republican date, whereas bronze coins of Rhodes of the second century AD have the inscription *didrachmon*, and we can see the detail of the relationship between denarius and cistophoric drachma in imperial times (it is a matter of dispute what, if any, fixed exchange rate existed between the two in Republican times), thanks to the coinage of Chios and several inscriptions. Chios, luckily for us, inscribed a whole series of denominations on its coins, basically according to two systems, the *assarion* or Roman as, for example **106** with the Greek inscription 'hemiassarion' or one and a half asses, and the *obolos* or local obol. It is clear from the weights and designs used that there was an equivalence of 1 obol = 2 asses, and, as there were 6 obols to the drachm, one would expect to find that 1 drachm = 12 asses. This is indeed the equivalence attested in an inscription from Ephesus of the early second century. Thus a drachm, in Asia, was tariffed at three-quarters of a denarius, and the principal coin, the cistophorus or cistophoric tetradrachm, was tariffed at three denarii. Although this seems very clear and neat, it should be added that it is not the whole story; different names could be applied to the same denomination (an as was also a *tetrachalkion*), while some scholars have argued that the exchange rate between cistophorus and denarius was later changed to 4 to 1.

The denarius in the empire

This survey of the silver currency of the different parts of the empire has tended to exaggerate the importance of the local silver as compared with the denarius. Yet it is implicit that the denarius was easily the most important silver coin, whose rôle in the empire became more and more vital; even in the second century BC, when its circulation was more restricted, it had been produced in greater quantity than any other coinage. As I have described, it became even more important as it first penetrated and later often took over as the principal circulating medium in more and more areas (*see* Fig. 3.1). The reason for its success seems to lie partly in the fact that, whether due to weight or silver purity, it usually contained rather more silver than the local coinages, which therefore tended to be confined to the areas where their circulation was enforced, whereas it was able to circulate almost everywhere.

Apart from the interest of the designs used (*see* chapter four), the only real alterations to the denarius during the whole period were in the decline of its silver fineness (*see* Fig. 6.2); otherwise it proved a remarkably stable coin for over 400 years. It had been struck at a very high fineness during most of the Republican period, although slight debasement (to 92%) had been made by Mark Antony in the 30s BC. In the early empire it remained fine, until Nero in AD 64 reduced its fineness to 93% (a reduction which required an analogous change to the coinage of Caesarea in Cappadocia), and the decline continued in the Flavian period under the emperor Vespasian (AD 69–79). Shortly after his accession, however, Domitian had restored the coinage to its early imperial purity (**88** is 98% silver: again this change was reflected in the provincial silver of Syria and Cappadocia), but this experiment lasted for only three years until AD 85, when the fineness was again reduced. It did, however, remain at the Neronian level, higher than under Vespasian, until the reign of Trajan. The next main reduction in fineness (to 89%) was made by Trajan in 107 (**89**). It was further reduced to about 84% in 148, and thereafter continued to slide during the second century, until in AD 195, early in the reign of Septimius Severus (**101**), it was again substantially reduced, to a little over 50%. A couple of years before, in AD 193, Pertinax had tried to reverse the trend (back to 87%), and the same kind of attempt was made by Macrinus in 217–18. These efforts seem to have been motivated by the moralistic desire of highly conservative emperors to restore the coinage to its previous condition, and did not succeed, presumably because the state simply could not afford them. Debasement continued, largely caused by the need to meet increasing – because of external, or particularly, civil wars – financial obligations from the stock of available and newly mined precious metal. Severus's debasement, in particular, may have been made more necessary by the recent exhaustion of the Spanish silver mines.

By this time, due to the falling fineness and the greatly

increased numbers of denarii being produced (*see* chapter six), the value of the denarius had sunk so much that its usefulness was greatly reduced. In response, a new larger silver coin was introduced, characterised by the radiate crown worn by the emperor and today often known as the 'radiate' or the 'antoninianus' (**104**), after the official name (Antoninus) of Caracalla, the emperor who first introduced it in about AD 215. These new coins were probably tariffed at 2 denarii, although they weighed only 1½ times as much as a denarius and hence they could be called *kibdelon argyrion* or 'tricky silver' (Dio 78.14.4). At first they were made for only a few years, but from AD 238 production was resumed and they replaced the denarius as the staple silver coin. Denarii continued to circulate for a little over ten years, but during the reign of Trajan Decius (AD 249–51) they were mostly withdrawn from circulation and many were reused as 'blanks' for reminting as radiates, for instance, (**114**) was struck over a denarius of Severus, as can be seen from the traces of lettering remaining on the reverse. Thereafter, denarii were still struck by later emperors, but only in tiny quantities and with a very restricted circulation; they may have played some more ceremonial role, and were in any case without any economic significance.

The aureus

During the whole imperial period the history of the denarius was parallelled by that of the gold coin, the *aureus*. During the Republic, gold had only been coined in times of emergency, like the Hannibalic War or the Sullan Civil War, presumably to eke out insufficient supplies of silver. From the time of Caesar, however, gold became a staple part of the Roman coinage, and it was coined regularly from 46–44 BC by Caesar at his own mint somewhere in Rome (**44**), presumably from the huge quantities of gold that he had won in his campaigns in Gaul and which he had seized from the Roman treasury in his entry in Rome (15,000 ingots). After his death in 44 BC, the various factions in the ensuing civil wars regularly coined large quantities of gold, and, like their denarii, these were produced throughout the Roman world and not just in Italy. This had several effects. Firstly, it established gold as a regular part of the monetary system. Secondly, it brought to an end the very few remaining local gold coinages, such as that of Ephesus in Asia. Thirdly, it established the circulation of gold throughout the empire. The aureus was, indeed, the only truly imperial coin of the Roman world; it was the sole gold coin in circulation, and it circulated freely everywhere, even in the otherwise closed province of Egypt.

Gold coinage was minted in large quantities throughout the first and second centuries, particularly late in the reign of Nero (**79**) and during the second century, when it has been estimated that something like one million new aurei were minted every year. Its fineness was always maintained at a very high standard (about 99%) until the end of the period, and debasement of the gold occurred only in about 253. The weight of the aureus, however, gradually declined, more or less in step with the debasement of the denarius, although the absence of a close correlation is slightly unexpected. It has been thought that other factors were at work, for instance that alterations in both the weight of the aureus and the volume of its production were made to compensate for changes in the relative price of gold and silver, but such a sophisticated view of Roman monetary control has not won general acceptance. The first main reduction (from 7.85 grams to 7.20) was in AD 64; the weight was increased with Domitian's reform of 82 to 7.70, but fell slightly with his second reform of 85 to 7.50. It fell again in Trajan's reign to 7.20, after which it remained stable until the third century. From 215, however, it rapidly declined and from that date some rare multiple pieces were made, characterised by the presence of a radiate crown, for example for Caracalla and Gordian III.

The value of the aureus was fixed at 25 denarii in the first two centuries AD, and probably remained at the same rate thereafter. It has been suggested that the substantial debasement of the denarius by Severus would have rendered this equivalence untenable, and that the value of the aureus must have risen in terms of denarii. Against this must be set the fact that a famous passage of Cassius Dio (55.12.3), which is the latest known text to give the equation 1 aureus = 25 denarius, appears to use the present tense. Dio was writing no earlier than about 215–16, and perhaps as late as the reign of Severus Alexander (222–35).

Production of the aureus was, from the middle of the reign of Augustus (15 BC), centralised at the principal imperial mint, initially at Lyon in France and from the later first century at Rome. Like denarii, issues were occasionally made in the provinces in times of civil war (AD 68–69 and 193–197), but basically the provision of precious metal coinage was centralised, exclusively so in the case of gold and, as has been seen, less so in the case of silver.

Provincial bronze coinage in the Republic

The bronze coinage, however, shows something of the same pattern, whereby centrally produced coins tended to replace local ones, but centralisation was much less developed than in the case of the silver or gold. The bronze coinage produced during the Republic at the mint of Rome has already been described. It circulated primarily in Italy and Sicily, but also in Spain and on a small scale in Africa. In all four areas it was supplemented by local bronze coinages, in inverse proportion to the amount of Roman coinage in circulation. Even in Italy there were a few – if tiny – issues of civic bronze down to the first century, for example that of Velia, and even, in the case of Paestum, until the reign of Tiberius (70). In Sicily, as finds in excavations show, there was a rather larger circulation of local bronze; in addition the Roman governors of Sicily seem to have minted their own specifically Romano-Sicilian issues. In Spain, there were large emissions from a number of communities, both of bronze coins corresponding to the Iberian denarii, for example (37) minted at Saetabi, and, further south, of individual city issues with their own types. All these coins used Roman denominations, but there was no attempt there, or indeed in Italy, to adhere to Roman weight standards and the coins were often minted at much lower weights. The relative importance of Roman and Spanish bronze can be seen from the coins found in modern excavations, which suggest that local bronze accounted for over half the bronze in circulation, or even more in civilian settlements (as opposed to military camps) and particularly in the more southerly and easterly parts of the peninsula, where local coinage was on a very much more restricted scale.

In Africa during the Republic, only a tiny quantity of Roman bronze seems to have circulated, since it is only rarely found there today, and hardly any local bronze was minted there in the first century of Roman rule. The bulk of the bronze currency of the area consisted of the large issues of the earlier Carthaginian and Numidian coins which continued to circulate in large numbers until the imperial period, in contrast to the Carthaginian gold and silver, which had been immediately demonetised after the conquest of 146 BC; presumably some way of accommodating them to the Roman monetary system was found. In the same way, the bronze currency of nearby Cyrenaica consisted of the mass of Ptolemaic bronze coins which had previously been struck and had been in circulation there.

In the eastern part of the Roman world, however, Roman bronze, like the silver, did not circulate during the Republic. There, the great mass of locally minted Hellenistic civic and regal issues continued to circulate and indeed to be struck after Roman annexation.. These coins generally show little or no signs of Romanisation; we are almost completely in the dark about their denominations, and their designs continued as before, usually making it almost impossible to establish which pieces were minted under Roman authority and which were earlier. There are just a few exceptions before the period of the civil wars of the late Republic, one of which occurred in Bithynia (north-east Asia Minor). There several cities such as Bithynion (41) produced a series of bronze coins with the seated figure of the goddess Roma, explicitly labelled, and the name of the Roman governor on the reverse. It may be no accident that this series begins in the 50s BC, the date at which signs of Romanisation were appearing elsewhere – on the cistophori of neighbouring Asia. Similarly, at about the same time in Syria and Palestine, some coins were minted in the aftermath of the Roman settlement of 63 BC with clear allusions to Rome; the bronze coinage of Gadara, for instance, boldly proclaims its date, using the Roman provincial era (e.g. "year one of Rome", *L A Romes*), while a portrait of Gabinius, the financial reformer of the region, appears on a recently discovered coin of Nysa.

This was the situation up to the period of the Civil Wars of the late Republic. These wars saw two developments. First, there seems to have been an increase in the quantity of bronze, especially large bronze, coins minted; occasionally these have the name of some Roman officer, and are presumably to be interpreted as coins minted to pay, in some way, for the expenses of the wars. Second, the most powerful leaders, although they probably continued to use mainly the anonymous civic bronzes, began to mint their own bronze coinage. Sextus Pompey in Sicily continued the bronzes of his father (the famous Pompey), adapting the traditional design of the head of Janus to include his father's features (47), and in response to this Octavian completely dropped the old typology and minted coins with the portrait of his adoptive father, Julius Caesar, sometimes accompanied by his own (48). A large number of such coins was made somewhere in north Italy, and several more similar issues were made in Gaul, at Narbonne, Arausio (?), Lyon and Vienna. Mark Antony also literally stamped his authority on the bronze coinage. In the parts of Syria which he had given to Cleopatra under the notorious "donations of Alexandria", his portrait often accompanies hers, and sometimes appeared on its own. Of even greater interest, however, is the coinage he produced some time after the pact he made at Brundisium with Octavian. This, traditionally known as the "fleet coinage", was produced by three prefects of Antony. Its interest lies partly in that its largest denomination was the first bronze sestertius of the Roman world (**52**), but mainly in the fact that the three groups were produced with identical designs in three different locations, two in Greece and one (of Bibulus) much further east, in Syria or Cyprus. This is signficant because it demonstrates that a kind of uniform imperial currency (which otherwise was not adopted by Rome until about AD 300) was possible then.

The Augustan reform of the bronze coinage

Antony's reform shows that one of the options open to the emperor Augustus, after his defeat of Antony and establishment of sole rule, was the establishment of a universal imperial currency. In a famous passage, written by the historian Dio in the third century but set in 29 BC, Maecenas, Augustus's great adviser, suggests that consideration should be given to the idea that the cities should not have "their own" weights, measures and coins, but "ours" (52.30.9). It is often pointed out that this passage can only prove that such ideas were current in the third century, but, as Antony's coinage shows, there is no reason to suppose that such proposals could not have been made earlier. Indeed, it seems something of a coincidence that in about the very same year (29 BC), Augustus (or Octavian, as he was called before 27 BC) inaugurated a very large and uniform bronze coinage for the east (**59**). Probably minted in Asia, it circulated widely throughout Asia and Syria, and must have been produced in very large quantities, to judge from the number of pieces which turn up today (particularly the smaller denominations). However, for reasons which remain obscure, this coinage was abandoned about ten years later, and Asia continued with only its locally produced bronze.

Although this Asian experiment was abandoned, it had one far-reaching legacy in that it provided Augustus with the metrological pattern for his permanent reform of the western imperial bronze coinage. The Asian coins had used different base metals, brass and bronze, for the different denominations, following the practice of other areas of Asia in the earlier first century BC, and in this respect the western reform followed suit, also copying the weights and general appearance of the eastern coins. The new structure of the coinage was as follows:

sestertius	(**60**)	= 4 asses	brass
dupondius	(**61**)	= 2 asses	brass
as	(**62**)		copper
semis		= ½ as	brass
quadrans	(**63**)	= ¼ as	copper

What was the purpose of this reform, which set the pattern for the imperial base metal coinage of the next 250 years? The answer is not obvious. The reform achieved three things, although it is not clear what weight, if any, should be given to each as a motive. Firstly, by resuming the fairly frequent (even if not regular) production of bronze coinage, it would have relieved the shortage of bronze which had prompted the imitations of Republican bronze in the first century BC. The everyday need for small change would have been helped even more by the production of the smallest denomination, the quadrans, in large quantities, although the first quadrantes were not struck for some two decades after the reform. Secondly, it effectively halved the weight standard of the bronze coinage, since the as was now about half the weight it had been in Republican times, and presumably this would have brought a saving of bullion costs of some sort to the government. The standard – and indeed the metal, copper – used for the as was in fact exactly the same as that of the disastrous experimental lightweight asses of about 90 BC. Presumably their introduction succeeded this time because a greater confidence was engendered in the new coins by the addition of the impressive new glittering yellow brass coins (the first syllable of the Latin word for brass, *orichalcum*, was, as the Romans were aware, phonetically like the word for gold, *aurum*), and by the probable revaluing of earlier bronze coins by twice their face value. Thirdly, the purchasing power of base metal coinage was greatly increased, not just by the revaluation of old coins, but also by the production of new coins of a much higher denomination than had previously been made, namely the dupondius and sestertius. If it is correct to think that payments to the state (e.g. taxes) had to be made in silver, then the new ability of the state to make many of its payments in the new base metal would have provided a clear financial incentive for the reform. It must, however, be admitted that all three lines of explanation are purely hypothetical; the answer may well be quite different.

The reform was brought in by Augustus at the mint of Rome, probably in 23 BC, although this date has been the subject of much argument, and dates in the teens have also been put forward, and the actual reform was probably supervised by the moneyer Cn Calpurnius Piso, son of the consul of the year. At first only the three large denominations were struck, and not all of them were minted every year. The coins were, however, struck in very large numbers to judge from their survival today, even though their main area of circulation concentrated on Italy and Sicily and was not much different from that of the Republican bronze from the mint of Rome. The currency of Spain and Africa continued to be made up predominantly of earlier local coins, supplemented by the fairly large quantities of local bronze minted in the two areas under Augustus and Tiberius. In Sicily, too, local issues were made at the same time, but on a much smaller scale, and the cities of Sicily supplemented the local civic issues by occasionally countermarking Augustan bronze coins from Rome and issuing them as their own. In Gaul there were still in circulation large quantities of local Celtic bronze, which had seen a great surge of production at the time of Caesar's campaigns, and to these were added various issues of bronze from Roman colonies. One of these, that of Nemausus (Nimes) (64), was clearly manipulated by Augustus in the same way that some Greek issues had been manipulated in Republican times to provide a substantial Roman coinage, for huge quantities of bronze were minted at Nemausus from the beginning of Augustus's reign to a date near its end. These Nemausan coins formed a very large proportion of the currency of Gaul, particularly until 10 BC when another colonial coinage, that of Lugdunum, the modern Lyon (which had by then become the empire's principal gold and silver mint), was utilised in a similar way. Unlike the coinage of Nemausus, however, which had been made of bronze and to its own weight standard, the new coins minted at Lyon (and perhaps also from an auxiliary mint) followed the metrological pattern of the reformed base metal coinage of Rome and continued to be made as such until production ceased early in the reign of Tiberius (AD 14–37).

The end of local bronze in the west

From that time, therefore, the only major base metal mint in the western part of the empire was at Rome, and large quantities of coin were minted, particularly the *Providentia* asses of the deified Augustus minted by Tiberius (67), the Agrippa asses minted by Gaius (AD 37–41), and the Minerva asses of Claudius I (AD 41–54) (74). Such coinage came to play an even more important part in the base metal currency of areas outside Italy, although their supply was clearly not sufficient to meet demands, and large numbers of imitations were manufactured (75). At first these imitations were largely confined to Gaul, but in the reign of Claudius they became more widespread, being made in Gaul, the new province of Britain, Spain, possibly Africa, and even, on a small scale, in Italy. The shortage of bronze coinage in several of these areas was exacerbated by the cessation of local civic bronzes. Local issues in Spain, Sicily and Africa continued until the reign of Tiberius in the case of Sicily and Africa, or Gaius for Spain; there is additionally one civic coinage for Claudius, from Ebusus, the modern Ibiza. From this time, however, local coinage in the western part of the empire ceased, in complete contrast to the east where it continued and indeed increased in importance throughout the next two hundred years.

How are we to explain the ending of local issues in the west? Two explanations have been put forward. On the one hand, it is argued that, although local issues reached a peak under Augustus, they were uneconomic and gradually declined thereafter, becoming rarer and rarer until they petered out in the reign of Gaius. The opposing view sees the hand of state intervention, and suggests that the Roman authorities ordered, for some reason, that they should cease. The Romans could obviously take drastic steps with minting and circulation practice if they wished, as the contemporary case of newly invaded Britain demonstrates; all the ancient British mints were closed down, and their productions were rapidly demonetised in the areas under direct Roman control (as opposed to the client kingdoms). In the case of Spain, particularly, state intervention seems most likely, when the cessation of local coins is seen against the production of imitations of Claudian coins which immediately ensued. The question of whether these imitations were official or private has already been raised. In this case, if they were official and made in the civic mints whose local products had just ceased, then there can be no doubt that the change from one sort of coin to the other was officially instigated. On the other hand, if the imitations were made privately outside the mint, then the argument that coinage petered out because it was uneconomic to produce loses its force. This dilemma, which could apply equally to Britain and (if imitations really were made there) to Africa, seems to make it more reasonable to think that the western local bronze coinages were brought to an end as a matter of policy. Why this should have been so is not clear; it was, however, a moment when there was a certain amount of regulation of the coinage, for instance the

PLATE 1

1 (X$\frac{1}{2}$)

2 (X$\frac{1}{2}$)

3 (X$\frac{1}{2}$)

PLATE 2

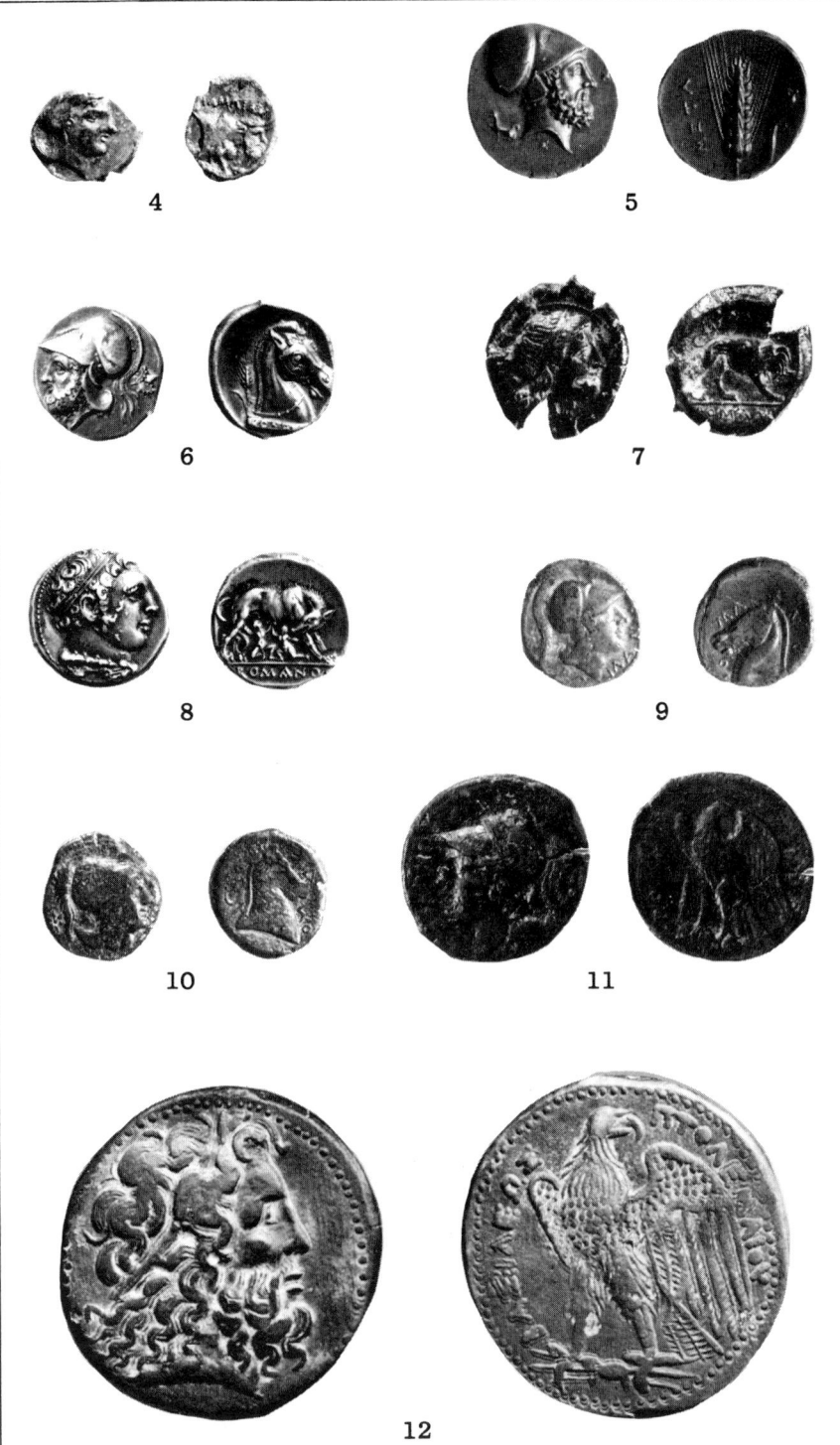

4

5

6

7

8

9

10

11

12

PLATE 3

13

14

15

16

PLATE 4

17

18

19

20

21

22

23

24

25

26

27

PLATE 5

28

29

30

31

32

33

34

35 (X2)

PLATE 6

36

37

38

39

40

41

42

43

44

45

PLATE 7

46

47

48

49

50

51

52

53

54

55

PLATE 8

Detail from Sword of Tiberius.
Department of Greek and Roman Antiquities, British Museum.

57

56

58

Augustus: Blacas Cameo.
Department of Greek and Roman Antiquities, British Museum.

senate decreed that all bronze coins with the hated image of the emperor Gaius, whose memory was officially obliterated after his death, should be melted down (Dio 60.22.3). The reasons for ending the local bronzes, however, are not clear, unless it is to be seen in the context of the option (discussed above) of imposing a universal coinage on the empire.

The problem of the shortage of small change in the west was not solved until late in the reign of Nero (AD 54–68), when large quantities of base metal were produced. In this reform, Nero made several experiments, such as making asses out of brass, dropping the letters SC from the coinage, and putting value marks such as II for dupondius (83) and S for semis on the coinage. These experiments were quickly abandoned, however, and the coinage resumed its previous course; the only permanent change was that from this time the dupondius was usually marked by the presence of a radiate crown on the emperor's portrait (83). This would have been of great practical help in enabling the populace to distinguish between the two similarly sized coins (the dupondius and the as), although it had divine overtones which may have made it distasteful to an emperor like Hadrian (AD 117–138), who therefore abandoned it for a time. A second (in this case, semi-permanent) reform by Nero was to establish a branch mint at Lyon, producing coins which were to all intents and purposes identical to those from Rome; only stylistic details allow modern numismatists to distinguish them. Once again this change should perhaps be interpreted as a move towards giving the whole western empire the same coins to use. The new Lyon mint relieved the shortage of bronze coin (imitations ceased) and provided virtually all the small denomination coins circulating in the west. Its production continued intermittently for some fifteen years until the reign of Vespasian (AD 69–79: 87) when it ceased.

Huge issues of asses in particular were minted in the later part of the first century; after the closure of the mint at Lyon in AD 78 these were all minted at Rome. The system of distribution from the mint to the provinces can be seen from the case of Britain. There are three cases where certain coins turn up plentifully in Britain, but rarely elsewhere. These are the asses of Domitian minted in AD 85–86, some rare asses of Nerva (AD 96–98) with a figure of Neptune, and the famous Britannia asses of Antoninus Pius (94) – there were corresponding pieces for the other three members of his imperial family. These three are either exclusively or overwhelmingly found in Britain, perhaps because they were minted at a local British branch mint, but more probably because they were minted at Rome and then shipped to Britain where they remained in circulation. Further evidence for the shipping of coins to Britain from Rome can perhaps be seen in the coins of Claudius with the countermark PROB, which remarkably occurs only in Italy and Britain, or from the pattern of circulation of third-century sestertii, for example those of Severus Alexander (AD 222–35), which are common in Italy and Africa, but hardly ever found in Britain. But, if the distribution of some bronze coins straight from the mint seems reasonably clear, it is an open question how much this system of supply applied to other coins. It seems likely for some of them, probably in conjunction with the recycling of old coin (*see* chapter five).

During the second and early third centuries, there was little change to the base metal currency of the west, although at some time, perhaps in the late first century, all the earliest imperial coins (of Augustus to Nero) had been demonetised. The metal to make the coins gradually changed, and the percentage of zinc in the brass coins gradually declined, being replaced by lead. This decline may be accounted for by the loss of zinc which takes place when earlier brass coins are melted down and then reminted. A more significant shift, however, took place in the pattern of denominations. An increasing emphasis was put on the production of sestertii from the reign of Trajan (AD 98–117) onwards (**90**). By the reign of Commodus (AD 180–92) dupondii and asses had become very rare. Semisses with the emperor's portrait were rare after the first century, and the last were minted under Antoninus Pius (AD 138–61); there was, however, a production of semisses (**96**) and quadrantes with anonymous designs until the reign of Antoninus Pius, when the minting of pieces smaller than the as stopped. Moreover, emphasis on the largest denomination, the sestertius, is all the more clear, if, as seems likely, a number of asses were made only for ceremonial purpose, for distribution to the populace at the new year.

Bronze coinage in the eastern empire

The picture of base metal coinage in the eastern part of the empire was completely different. There, with minor exceptions such as Cyprus from the late second century AD, bronze from the mint of Rome did not circulate, and the base metal currency was made up of the individually small but numerous issues of the Greek cities, for example Laodicea in Asia Minor (**66**). Many of these cities minted coins, more than a hundred under Augustus, after whose long reign there was something of a decline.

However, the number increased rapidly in the second century up to a peak of some two hundred in the early third century (compare Fig. 3.2 with 3.3). This increase is to be explained partly by a simple increase in the numbers of cities issuing coins, but also by the spread of civic issues to unfamiliar areas, such as the Danubian provinces and the more remote inland areas of Asia Minor.

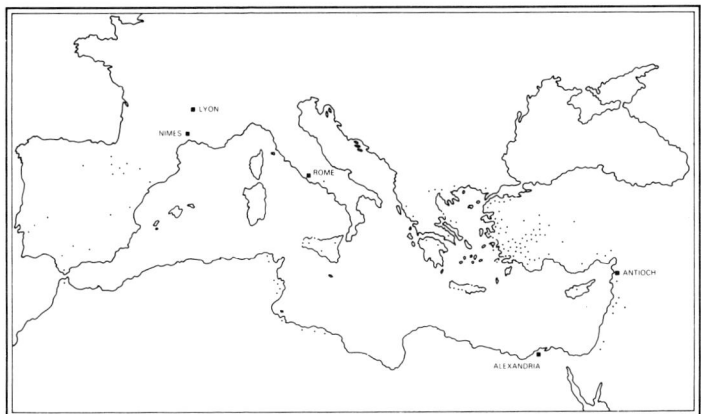

FIG. 3.2 *Imperial and Civic Mints under Augustus*

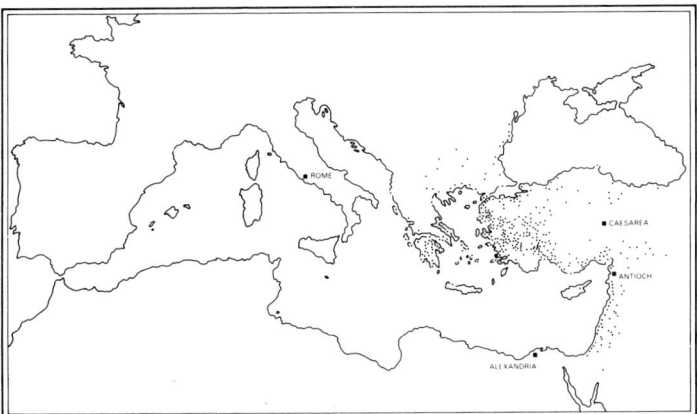

FIG. 3.3 *Imperial and Civic Mints in the Early Third Century*

At first these local issues were small and unimpressive, merely continuations in many cases of the bronze coinage of the Hellenistic period. There was little attempt to follow the pattern of the coinage produced in the west, although two areas, Thrace and Bithynia (north-west Asia Minor) are notable not so much for their use of brass, which had already been used since the middle of the first century BC, as for the production of large coins with long inscriptions, clearly imitating the general appearance of coins struck at Rome. From the end of the first century, however, the coins regularly came to be made at a larger size, for example, **91** of Trajan from Ephesus, and often in a range of denominations; very often the smaller of these did not have the emperor's head (the so-called "pseudo-autonomous" issues). There was still, however, no general attempt to make the coins look like Roman coins, and indeed in the early third century a few cities produced very large coins (so-called "medallions") at the size and weight far in excess of the Roman sestertii, for example, (**103**) a coin of Caracalla from Laodicea. At the very end of the civic coinage in the middle of the third century, there was a tendency for the coins both to include a decreasing amount of expensive zinc in favour of the cheaper lead, and to shrink in size, while, due to inflation, their value increased. For instance, the coins of Sparta, which mention their values, show a slump from a four as coin of Commodus (AD 180–92) weighing 10 grams to a four as coin of Gallienus (AD 253–68) weighing only about 5 grams. In a similar way, coins in Asia Minor were countermarked with numerals to give them higher value.

Exactly why a particular city chose to mint at a given time, and why its issue was of a particular size is not clear. Sometimes a connection has been seen with the travels of an emperor. For instance it has been thought that the journey of Caracalla across Asia Minor in AD 214/5 can almost be plotted from the cities which might be thought to have minted coins in response to his visit. However, a convincing case cannot be made, since only a maximum of eleven city issues can realistically be associated with his journey. Even if imperial presences could sometimes lead to civic issues, as they clearly did sometimes, for example for Caracalla at Pergamum, this explanation can only account for a tiny minority of city issues. We can get some idea of the oddity of the pattern of issues both by looking at the places which minted, and at the pattern of issues at a given city. Thanks to an inscription found a few years ago (*JRS* 1975, 64) we are lucky to have a list of all the communities in one conventus or sub-district of the Roman province of Asia in the first century, that of Sardis. We can compare this with the coinage minted there, and indeed with the relative importance of the communities as given by Pliny in his listing of the same area:

No. of communities:	28 or 29
No. which coined:	12
No. of 'important' communities:	8
No. which coined:	5
No. of 'unimportant' communities:	20 or 21
No. which coined:	7

These figures show clearly, first that the total number of communities which coined at all was relatively small in comparison with all that existed, and, second that, while there was a tendency for the more important centres to produce coinage, the relationship between coinage and (economic) importance is far from being so simple; moreover, in some districts, the coinage of the conventus centre or capital itself is sometimes overshadowed by some other city, for example Alabanda or Synnada.

Secondly, we can look at the pattern of coinage at an individual city. It is clear that not only was coinage usually on a small scale since sometimes only a single pair of dies was used, but that it was also intermittent. For instance, the coinage of the commercial centre of Hierapolis in Asia was, from the second century, apparently produced only once every twenty years, and there was only one really large issue, under Elagabalus in 221, struck in commemoration of the neocorate or award to the city of the right to build a temple in honour of the emperor. The coinage of the more important city of Sardis is slightly more frequent (struck on average once every ten years), but still only patchy and on a very small scale, with never more than a handful of dies. In particular there was a twenty-year gap in production from 175, a period which we know from other sources to have been one of great prosperity.

It is these two features of civic coinage, its irregularity and the volatility of its scale of production, that have defied most attempts to find a single convincing general explanation for its issue. The coins themselves are of little help, as their inscriptions reveal little of the motives for their minting. The only theme which recurs at all regularly is that of benefaction. The benefaction is usually the specific one of an individual's provision of the coinage to the city from his own means under the system of "liturgies", whereby a whole range of civic duties and expenditure would be undertaken by prominent, and rich, citizens. Sometimes the benefaction in question may have been the provision of coinage for distribution to the populace. This seems most clear from the analogy of the late Republican coinage of

Paestum in Italy, where a number of helpful inscriptions survive. One of them records, together with the representation of a coining scene, that SP DD SS MIL, *sua pecunia dono dedit senatus sententia milia*: "he gave as a gift from his own money, as authorised by the senate" – of Paestum – "a thousand (sestertii)". Another refers, with her portrait, to a woman called Mineia, who is known from inscriptions to have been a benefactress of Paestum. Together with the constantly differing titles of those who sign Paestan coins (as well as the woman and magistrates of different sorts, there are a priest and two 'patrons'), these examples suggest that at least some of the civic coinage was produced for distribution. No doubt other local events, such as the holding of games and festivals (which so often provide the designs), imperial visits or assize sessions would have increased the need for coinage and might have thus prompted the issue of new coin. Nor, indeed, should we underestimate the desire for prestige as a motive for coinage. This, together with profit, is given as the motive for the introduction of bronze coinage at Sestos in Greece in the second century BC (*OGIS* 339.44). Both motives may also have operated under the empire. Moreover, the reasons for the absence of coinage at some periods may well be as important as the reasons for its production at others. If, indeed, coinage was often an imposition on rich citizens, there may well have been a reluctance to undertake it; one legend at Mylasa records how the person who had proposed the coinage had paid for it: *psephisamenos Klaudios Melas anetheke*. Additionally, there may have been a lack of a suitable 'workshop' (*see* chapter two) to produce it.

The reasons behind the minting of provincial civic issues are, then, not clear, but seem to lie more in the realm of local rather than Roman needs. Although it seems likely that, particularly in the third century, Roman officials must have used some of these coins for their needs (such as the Severan coins from southern Greece, which appear to have been sent from there to Syria with auxiliary troops), they also minted some specifically Roman coinages for themselves. The most important of these was the bronze coinage of Antioch, which was reformed at the same time as the silver in 5BC, and thereafter comprised coins with Latin legends around the emperor's portrait, and on the back the letters SC in a laurel wreath (**65**). Initially, under Augustus, branch mints may also have been used (e.g. in Cyprus), but thereafter the coinage was concentrated in Antioch. The coinage did not use the brass and copper denominations introduced at Rome and used twenty years earlier in Asia (**59**), but consisted of two denominations made of bronze, one weighing about 15 grams and the other a half piece, weighing about 8; perhaps these represented asses and semisses, or dupondii and asses. The coinage was minted intermittently, but in fairly large quantities from the time of Augustus to the middle of the second century, when it began to peter out. It was supplemented in the reigns of Vespasian and Trajan by brass coins, which were probably made in Rome and shipped out to Syria. The specifically "Roman" as opposed to local function of these coins can be seen not so much from the use of Roman types and Latin legends as from the countermarks which were put on the coins to validate them by the Roman legions (e.g. LEG VI). It is very noticeable that these countermarks concentrate on the SC bronze of Antioch rather than the other local coins produced in the area, and this suggests an official Roman (military) function for them, in much the same way that the concentration of Roman (as opposed to "celtic") bronzes in military camps in first-century Gaul suggests a similar function for them.

The collapse of the system

Thus, with the exception of the "Roman" coinage of Antioch (and a similar bronze coinage from Caesarea in Cappadocia), the base metal coinage of the east consisted of a mass of different civic issues. For some two hundred years, from about AD 40, the bronze currency of the two parts of the empire had been quite different in nature. During the third century, however, the pressure of increasing prices (*see* chapter six) began to bring a change from this varied and stable system to the more uniform but less stable coinage system of the late Empire. This transition took place as the result of two parallel tendencies. Firstly, inflation caused the cessation of bronze coinage and thereby eliminated the most marked difference between the currency of east and west. Secondly, the need to produce more and more of the by now very debased silver coins led to the establishment of new mints to produce them in the provinces, for example at Siscia, commemorated on a coin of Gallienus (**119**); these mints also started to produce gold coins as well, thus ending the previous monopoly of the mint at Rome.

The most important stage in this transitional process took place in the joint reign of Valerian and Gallienus (AD 253-60) and the sole reign of Gallienus (260–68). These years saw the setting up of several new mints in the provinces (*see* Fig. 7.1) to produce the staple silver coins of the empire. Such mints had, of course, existed previously, particularly during times of civil war, but only on an occasional basis and only coining irregularly, even in the case of Antioch, the most important. Mints were established in the Balkans, at Siscia (?AD 263: 119) and (briefly) at Viminacium (AD 253), in response to the need for supplies of cash to pay the large concentrations of troops stationed there against the threat of the Goths. For similar reasons, new mints were set up further north, at Milan (AD 259) and somewhere in Gaul (AD 255), perhaps at Trier, in this case in connexion with Gallienus's campaigns against the Germans. Further east, the main threat was from the Persian empire. As well as the mint at Antioch, a second eastern mint was established for a brief period, perhaps a couple of years, somewhere else in Syria. Another permanent mint, probably at Cyzicus, opened in about 266.

The case of Antioch is, however, perhaps the most interesting, as it seems to throw some light on Valerian's monetary policy. It has three interesting features. First of all, it began to coin gold (previously the sole prerogative of Rome), and to do so on an occasional but fairly substantial basis. Secondly, the only silver coins minted there were radiates; the earlier coinage of silver tetradrachms, which had been prolific right up to the reign of Valerian, was discontinued. Thirdly, and perhaps most interestingly, some (today very rare) coins show that Antioch began to mint bronze asses of the traditional Roman design, for example that of Gallienus (116), thus breaking with the previous practice of the east in general and Antioch in particular. In these ways, the mint of Antioch had begun to behave very like the mint of Rome, and, taken together with the establishment of new mints to produce radiates of basically the same appearance, it seems that Valerian wished to impose some unity on the diverse coinage of the empire.

One should not, however, press this hypothesis too far, since there certainly seems to have been no attempt to suppress or unify the eastern civic coinages. These coinages continued to be issued by a large number of cities, not as many as in the heyday of provincial civic coinage around AD 200, but nevertheless from about a hundred cities. Another factor, however, was to bring an end to these coinages, namely the general cessation of bronze coinage throughout the empire. This occurred at this time, either because the purchasing power of bronzes became negligible with their low denominations, or because the intrinsic value of the silver coin fell below the intrinsic value of the bronzes which were supposed to be of lower value. At Rome, production of bronze coins all but ceased in about AD 260, and in Gaul the usurper Postumus made no sestertii after the early 260s. At Antioch, the last issue of bronze was made in about 264; similarly, at Alexandria, the last bronzes were struck in Gallienus's twelfth regnal year (AD 264), while the civic issues of Greece, Asia and Syria rapidly disappeared at more or less the same time. Unfortunately it is not possible at the moment to date the decline of these coinages with any accuracy. During the reigns of Valerian and Gallienus there had been about a hundred issuing cities, but for the next emperor, Claudius II (268–70), and for Aurelian (270–75) there were only five, while the last civic coins of all were struck in the reign of Tacitus (275–76), by the solitary city of Perga in Asia (**127**). Clearly the real decline must have occurred somewhere in the reign of Gallienus, roughly at the same time that the other bronze coinages ended.

Thus by the middle of the third century, the coinage system of the late Republic and early empire, which for all its diversity and changes had been immensely stable for some four hundred and fifty years, had finally disappeared. Thereafter the nature of the coins and their system of production changed greatly, and, despite the superficial uniformity of the late imperial monetary system, it had none of the stability or permanence of its predecessor.

Chapter Four

Designs and propaganda

Coins and propaganda

The significance of the designs used on coins, particularly Roman imperial coins, has been a vexed question for a long time, particularly of recent years. There is, of course, a wide spectrum of possible views. At one extreme, it can be thought that coins are really only economic objects, and that the designs placed on them are just incidental: they were chosen by a minor government department and were little noticed and generally misunderstood by a population that was largely illiterate or incapable of comprehending their subtle symbolism. At the other extreme, it can be thought that the emperor himself was interested in choosing the designs used on his coins to promote the various features of his reign which he wished to bring to the attention of the whole population. We might characterise these opposing views as the 'economic' and the 'propaganda', even though the word 'propaganda' is usually avoided nowadays, in favour of milder terms like 'message' or 'persuasiveness'. Yet its use seems unexceptionable, provided that we strip it of its two main twentieth-century connotations, namely that of deliberate falsehood and that of a systematic programme for the orchestration of public opinion. Neither practice is appropriate for the Roman world, where attempts were naturally made to enhance the emperor's public image, but on a more piecemeal basis and generally based on more genuine claims.

We do know that at least some people in the ancient world were aware of the potential force of coin designs. The classic instance can be found in an inscription of the second century BC from Sestos in northern Greece. At one point the inscription mentions the city's adoption of its own coinage, and the first reason it gives for this adoption is "so that the design of the city should be recognised" (*OGIS* 339.44). Clearly it could be assumed at Sestos that its coins would be noticed and would bring prestige to the city. Much the same is true of a remark of Epictetus (in the second century AD), the force of which would be lost unless it was common ground that people looked at coins and attached moral values to them:

"Just as a banker or greengrocer cannot reject Caesar's coin, but, if you show it, is obliged to take it, whether he likes it or not, and give over what he is selling in exchange for it, so it is with the soul. When the good appears it immediately attracts, while the bad repels. The soul will never reject the clear appearance of goodness, no more than we should reject Caesar's coin" (Arrian, *Discourses of Epictetus* 3.3.3.).

Elsewhere we hear of the story of the man who was offered a coin of Nero, but preferred one of Trajan, despite the fact that the Neronian coin had a greater value (*id.* 5.17). In both cases, it is assumed that people would look at their coins, and make a moral judgement about their content. Except for acknowledged tyrants like Nero, "Caesar's coin" was generally appreciated as having a positive and compelling moral force.

Finally, there are some rare coins minted in the reign of Trajan at the cities of Ephesus and Tripolis, both in Asia, which deliberately draw attention to their designs – celebrations of Trajan's Parthian victory – with their inscriptions: *Neo(koros) De(mos) epechar(axe)*, "the neocorate people of Ephesus put the design on" (**91**), or *Theodoros B echaraxe Tri(politais)*, "Theodoros, magistrate for the second time, put the design on for the Tripolitans". This explicit drawing of attention to the reverse designs of the coins indicates their importance, and implies that they would be noticed. In a similar way, perhaps, two issues of rebel denarii of AD 68 use the design of coining tools in conjunction with the slogans of salvation and vengeance, (VOLKANVS VLTOR, "Vulcan the Avenger" on **85**), implying that their coinage would free them from and avenge them for the hateful images on the coinage of the tyrant Nero.

Of course the fact that it could be thought or intended that people would notice coin designs does not demonstrate that they did so. Yet there is some evidence that they did, although this evidence is rather patchy, and concerns different social groups. The clearest, but least important, case concerns mint officials, who certainly knew what earlier coins looked like, inasmuch as they sometimes copied them. This happened on numerous occasions: for example, under Augustus (the coins of the moneyer M Durmius), under Vespasian, under Trajan (the restored denarii), under Constantine (Constantine looking at heaven: **140**), and generally throughout the later fourth and fifth centuries (the contorniates). The fact that mint officials were aware of the appearance of coins, however, is neither surprising nor particularly important here; of much greater potential relevance are the passages in ancient authors where coins are actually described, as these could imply that important members of the higher social classes noticed coin designs. For the later empire we have Eusebius's explicit testimonies about two Constantinian coin designs: "He directed his likeness to be stamped on a gold coin with his eyes uplifted in the posture of prayer to God . . . this coin was current through the Roman world and was a sign of the power of divine faith" (4.15). "A coin . . . (had) on one side a figure of our blessed prince, with head closely veiled; the reverse showed him sitting as a charioteer drawn by four horses, with a hand stretched downward from above to receive him up to heaven" (4.73). There can hardly be any doubt that Eusebius had seen the coins in question (**140** and **148**).

Perhaps the most famous of these descriptions for the earlier period is in Dio (47.25.3): "On the coins which he struck, he [Brutus] impressed his own image, and a Cap of Liberty and two daggers, demonstrating from this and through the inscription that he, with Cassius, had freed their country". Despite the accurate description (**46**) and correct interpretation, it is sometimes thought that this, and other, less accurate, literary descriptions of coins are based on written sources, rather than from actual inspection of the coins. This of course may well be true inasmuch as, for instance, Dio's immediate source may have been a written one, but this hardly matters. Clearly a detailed knowledge of the coin was acquired by someone, but more importantly it was appreciated by a senator like Dio that coins could have such significance; it is not necessary for 'propaganda' to be effective for it to exist.

The third, and potentially most telling, sort of evidence comes from anecdotes, which imply a much greater awareness of a particular coin by the population at large. There are two good examples. One is the famous scene of Jesus. ' "Fetch me a silver piece. . . . Whose head is this, and whose inscription?" "Caesar's," they replied. Then Jesus said, "Pay Caesar what is due to Caesar, and pay God what is due to God." ' (Mark 12.15). The second comes from the late empire, where it is described how, in the reign of Julian, the people of Antioch demonstrated against the Emperor, "shouting . . . that his coinage had a bull [which it had: **158**], and that the world was overturned" (Socrates, *Hist Eccl.* 3.17).

It seems then reasonably clear that in the ancient world it was expected that coin designs would be noticed and that this expectation was at least sometimes fulfilled. Undoubtedly, it is true that what was most commonly noticed was the emperor's portrait, as it was regarded as a sign of sovereignty (see for example the story of Jesus, or the cases of Procopius and Perennis in chapter two), but the examples of Eusebius and Julian show that the reverse design was also noticed. It is, moreover, surely incorrect to draw too great a contrast between the 'message' of the portrait and the design on the reverse; both are aspects of the same 'message' and both have a moral value. The portrait focuses on the emperor, the reverse gives the reasons (either explicitly, in terms of specific achievements, or implicitly, in terms of qualities of the emperor and his regime) why he should be the object of such a focus. And, of course, this brings us back to the apparent opposition between the 'economic' and the 'propaganda' role of the coin, a distinction which blurs the interdependence of the two roles. A coin's economic validity depends a lot on the images it bears, for they threaten penalties against treason or sacrilege and thereby help protect the coin against abuse (*see also* chapter five). Similarly, the 'propaganda' element is enhanced by the economic role of the coin, since it interposes its message in all transactions between individuals, and forces them to acknowledge the position of the state or emperor, as the story of Jesus makes clear.

Thus there are good reasons for believing that coins had a 'propaganda' value, provided we do not use that word in its overladen modern sense. We should not, however, attempt to overestimate the importance of coins in this rôle, as compared with other more important methods of transmission of the public image of an emperor. These will have included portrait sculpture, monumental architecture (whether presenting particular achievements like victories or using more complex symbolic language, for instance on the Augustan monuments in Rome), inscriptions, speeches and, above all, ceremonies like the triumph in Rome, which will have clearly communicated to even the most humble, and no doubt found echoes in local festivals in the provinces. But how rigidly were all these means of influencing the popular appreciation of the emperor's public image controlled, whether by the emperor himself or his officials? Permission had to be sought for a temple to be dedicated to the emperor – and could be refused. In the case of a massive and important construction at Rome like the Forum of Augustus, we can hardly avoid the conclusion that the emperor was closely involved; indeed, it is sometimes thought that he personally composed the 'elogia' or tributes to famous men which adorned it, and we must imagine that he at least approved the rest of the design.

In the case of coinage, imperial interest is often presumed, and indeed there is some evidence for this. Literary sources often state that an emperor chose a particular coin design. Suetonius describes how Nero "set up statues of himself playing the lyre, and had a coin struck with the same design" (*Nero* 25), and the first passage of Eusebius above clearly implies that the designs were personally chosen by the emperor. Yet one should not perhaps take these statements too literally, as under any regime any action, however trivial, is often attributed to the leader, whether or not he was closely involved. It seems more likely that designs were submitted to the emperor, rather like the way that Alexander of Abonouteichos in Asia had not only asked the emperor permission to make coins, but to make coins with specific types (Lucian, *Alexander* 58). In a similar way it has been suggested that designs were chosen by the emperor's officials and offered with the intention of flattering him; this model of design selection, of course, also implies imperial approval, whether explicit or implicit, since a design would hardly be chosen unless it was appropriate to the known preferences of the emperor. When we look for actual instances of imperial control, however, they are exasperatingly elusive. The artistic improvement so noticeable on the coinage of Nero (82) or Domitian (88) may stem directly from these emperors' aesthetic sense or it may just reflect a more artistic cultural climate. So too with designs. The insistence on Domitian's coinage on the figure of the goddess Minerva (88) may well be the result of Domitian's personal predeliction for her; but, again, his preference was so well known that it would have made Minerva an obvious choice. In general, the actual involvement of the emperor seems likely on occasion but otherwise may have been rather more notional than contemporaries and modern commentators have assumed. And of course in a sense this does not really matter, since we must surely presume that it was recognised that coin types could be attributed to the emperor's personal choice; moreover, by looking at the public expressions of a regime – whatever the exact mechanism of their selection – we can still assess the public image of that regime, and attempt to understand how it wished to present itself.

It is probably a mistake to think of too rigid a control of the public image in antiquity, on the false modern analogy of, say, seventeenth and eighteenth-century France, where there was close supervision to ensure that the arts were used in harmony to extol the gloire of the king. Indeed there was even a special organisation, La Petite Académie (founded in 1663), which closely monitored and approved the designs and inscriptions used for statues, fountains, paintings, tapestries, even operas and poems, as well as for contemporary commemorative medals. Such close control indicates that such images were thought to be very significant, but the Roman world was not such a closely organised society as modern France. The typical picture of the way in which the Roman empire was run was that the emperor generally responded to specific stimuli from below (hence the importance of embassies to the emperor) and was not constantly initiating new empire-wide policies. By analogy, the model which sees the designs of imperial coinage chosen in a fairly unsystematic way to accord with the ideals of the emperor, whether or not they were actually approved by him, seems the most probable. Close imperial control seems even more unlikely, as will be seen, for the designs used by provincial cities, which seem to be the local idea of what was suitable.

The example of Augustus

What this means in practice can perhaps best be understood by examining the development of Roman coin design, paying particular attention to what appear to be crucial phases in it. The clearest instances of the 'propaganda' use of coin types come at times of severe political crisis or uncertainty. The desire to use coinage to convey slogans or ideas becames so pressing that the language of words and images is stridently simple and clear, as a glance at the coins produced in the civil wars of the late Republic or AD 68–69 will show. One of the most important instances of political uncertainty was the reign of Augustus, standing as it did at the transition between the Republic and empire. This was a crucial time when people did not really know what to expect, and it was essential for Augustus to indicate the sort of monarchical system he was establishing. His system was basically a combination of the absolute power of the divine kings of the eastern Mediterranean in the Hellenistic period and the moderating influence of his restoration of the Republican constitution and ideals (**55**); and the coinage too had to accommodate itself to both traditions.

The early development of Republican designs has already been briefly described in chapter two. In this phase there had been a change from the 'public' designs like Roma and the Dioscuri (**17–21**) to 'private' ones, related to the personal family of the moneyer (**29**). This change, which brought about the great variety of designs in Republican coinage, was virtually without precedent in the previous history of coinage. It is probably to be explained partly by the Gabinian law of 139, although the basic instability of the late Republican political system provided the underlying conditions under which the bold use of coin designs had a purpose, in contrast, for example, to the long period of peaceful stability in the second century AD, when they became bland. But while the changing 'private' designs of Republican coins were originally linked to the person of the moneyer, they rapidly came under the influence of the powerful military figures who started to dominate the late Republican scene. From the time of Marius, just before 100 BC, moneyers began to refer to the achievements of such men who were not related to them, but for whom they wished to proclaim their political support. By the middle of the first century, the coinage was dominated by allusions to Pompey (the three wreaths on (**33**) symbolise his African, Spanish and eastern triumphs), and the same was true under the dominate of Caesar (49 to 44 BC). Just before his death Caesar took the momentous step of having his portrait placed on the coinage (**45**); although it was a portrait in the traditional Roman manner, no contemporary observer could fail to connect his innovation with the practice of the Greek kings in the eastern Mediterranean who, from the time of Alexander the Great (336–323 BC), had used their portraits (which were in a different style, derived from that of Alexander) as symbols of sovereignty on their coinage. It was the legacy of these two features, portraiture and frequently changing designs, that set the scene for the large-scale and varied coinage of the thirteen years of civil war from Caesar's assassination until Octavian's victory. As with the coinage of other periods of civil crisis, the designs became far more easy to understand and their legends more explicit than their more allusive predecessors; for example, the victories which were simply and explicitly claimed, or the overt attempts at legitimisation, such as Octavian's use of the portrait of his adoptive father, Caesar, or justification, such as Brutus's design of the cap of liberty and the daggers (**46**).

This was the character of the coinage at the time of Octavian's final victory at Actium in 31 BC. It was peppered with claims to his various victories, achievements and the honours he had received (honours appropriate to humans, heroes, and gods) combined with his personal portrait (**54**), which was rendered not in a traditional Roman style like Caesar's, but in the manner of the Hellenistic kings. The unusual absence of any inscription made a direct link with the coins of such kings. But Octavian, as is well known, stepped back from establishing a regime for himself along the lines of contemporary monarchies, and wished to combine his personal power with the restoration of the Republican constitution. His coinage clearly mirrors this policy; (55) vividly shows him in the act of raising or restoring the Republic. There are two clear ways in which he moderated his personal image to accommodate it with the more restrained conventions of the traditional Roman outlook. Firstly, all allusions to divine or heroic (i.e. more than human) attributes were removed from his images, including those on coins; no longer was he shown naked, in the heroic style, or with divine symbols like Jupiter's thunderbolt (54), but just as a human, fully clothed, and performing only human activities. It is interesting to note that this 'human' image of the emperor was used for objects of mass circulation like coins, whereas the 'divine' image persisted in more educated classes, such as in poems for literary circles or on presents for those in the higher ranks of the army, where presumably it could be the object of a more subtle appreciation and would not be misinterpreted. A very clear example occurs for the celebration of the victory of Tiberius over the Vindelici in 15 BC. On coins (56) Tiberius is shown with his brother Drusus presenting laurel branches, the symbol of his victory, to the emperor, who is shown wearing a toga and seated on a magistrate's chair. In contrast, the same scene is shown on the scabbard of the sword, which was probably for presentation (see Plate 8). On the scabbard's decoration Augustus is likened to the god Jupiter by being portrayed half-naked, and seated on a divine throne. Such 'divine' representations were confined to such objects with limited circulation. Similarly they can be found on, for instance, cameos (see Plate 8, where Augustus is again likened to Jupiter), but never appeared on coins.

Secondly, Augustus changed his portrait from one based on the Hellenistic royal tradition to one based on the ideals of the classical Greek city state, by copying the famous Doryphoros, "spear carrier", of Polycleitus, which was known at the time as the archetype of the "serious and pious man". This new portrait of him as the first citizen also appeared on coins (57), although curiously there was not the same definite break between the two as in sculpture, but more of a gradual transition over the first ten years or so of his reign.

This manipulation of his image should warn us against supposing that his portrait was intended to be a closely realistic representation of his actual appearance. Indeed his biographer Suetonius has left us a description of his appearance: "his appearance was distinguished and graceful . . . he had clear bright eyes . . . few teeth, which were small and dirty . . . his hair was yellowish and slightly curly, his eyebrows met and his nose jutted out then turned inwards . . . on his body were spots, birthmarks and callouses . . . he sometimes limped and suffered generally from a weak constitution" (*Augustus* 79–82). A glance at his portrait, whether in the round or on coins, illustrates the contrast: his portrait was not supposed to be a 'photograph', but to embody his own political ideals. In addition to his choice of a particular imagery, we can easily see the lack of realism in his portrait from its failure to show him ageing during a forty-four year reign; Suetonius's may be a description of him in old age, but we should never have guessed from his portraits, which can be fairly accurately dated on coins, that he had progressed from the age of thirty-six (**57**) to seventy-five (**58**). His portrait gradually matured, but remained essentially youthful. This too was deliberate. After a time of tremendous and prolonged crisis, his unchanging portrait was a symbol of stability and his perpetual youthfulness held out the promise that this stability would endure.

As well as the legacy of portraiture, Augustus had inherited the explicit use of designs and inscriptions from the civil wars, and he filled his coinage with similarly direct references to the achievements which contributed to the power of his personal position. It has often been noticed that there is a substantial link between the coin designs of his reign and the content of the *Res Gestae Divi Augusti*, an inscription recording "The Achievements of the Divine Augustus", possibly prepared by Augustus himself during his reign, and published posthumously by being set up all over the empire. Both the inscription and the coins recorded, for instance, the end of the civil wars, referring indirectly to Augustus's defeats of Sextus Pompey and Antony, and propagated his favourite political slogans: the restoration of the Republic, and with it peace and liberty. The subsequent history of the reign, as seen through his eyes, dwells on two themes: his military and diplomatic successes (the capture of Armenia, or the recovery of the Parthian and Gallic standards), and his financial generosity to the state: how he had often helped the treasury, paying for road construction or public entertainments out of his own pocket. These achievements were rewarded by a series of extravagant honours: the title "Augustus", the setting of a laurel branches and an oak crown (awarded for saving citizens) outside his house, the golden shield (awarded for his *virtus* or bravery) or the title *Pater Patriae*, "Father of his Country" included in the legend (**58**). In such respects the similarity of content between his coinage and the Res Gestae inscription is quite clear. While we should see them both as different aspects of the propagation of the achievements and values which justified and enhanced the supreme position of Augustus, it is equally clear that the coins did this in a completely unsystematic way. For most of the reign there was no careful balancing of designs, giving appropriate emphasis to different ideals. Rather, it seems that a particular design was used, sometimes in conjunction with others, and then after a certain time it was replaced with another suitable one, emphasising some other ideal or achievement. The only truly systematic theme common to all aspects of the public image, whether the designs of coins, the Res Gestae or the emperor's portrait, is the emphasis on the person of the emperor, to the almost total exclusion of anyone else. His allies and supporters, to whom he owed virtually everything, were almost entirely ignored.

The development of designs during the empire

In many ways Augustus set the pattern for the subsequent imperial coinage. His immediate successors modelled their portrait on his, in the attempt to legitimise their position. They needed to stress their connexion with him both to maintain the idea of monarchy, by recalling his powerful position as the founder of a dynasty, and to support their claim to be his successor, since they were often rather distant relations. More explicitly, they stressed their connection with him by issuing coins posthumously in his name, and Tiberius, for instance, emphasised his claim to the succession by minting enormous quantities of coins in the name of his adoptive father, Divus Augustus Pater (**67**). The same reason explains the large number of family portraits which appear, particularly in the reigns of Gaius, (such as **72** of his mother Agrippina the Elder), and of Claudius; which stressed their connexion with Augustus and their claim to continue his dynasty.

With the reign of Nero, however, there was a break with the Augustan tradition. Two developments are apparent, firstly a new artistic quality with more imaginative perspectives and higher relief and, secondly, a much greater realism. Just as we can imagine ourselves really looking at a triumphal arch (**82**) – compare the merely schematic representations of earlier reigns, such as those of Claudius (**73**) – so we can actually see Nero getting older and witness the prodigious change in his physical appearance which took place in the brief fourteen years of his reign (**78** to **79**). There was no attempt to conceal the fact that he was getting older and (considerably) fatter. Paradoxically, at the same time that this realism appeared, he was also depicting himself with divine features. Whether Nero wished to see himself as a living god or not is unclear; but, while he gave himself some mortal characteristics, he also adopted some divine ones. On the coinage, the two divine features are the *aegis* (**82**), a goatskin, worn on the shoulder, with a head of Medusa and her hair of snakes, which was the badge of both Jupiter and Minerva, and the crown of rays (**83**), which was an emblem of divinity since, when deified, one shone from heaven like a star. Both emblems had been worn by Hellenistic kings, some of whom had presented themselves as gods, and the radiate crown had been used to denote the divinity of Augustus, after his posthumous deification. Despite some scholarly hesitation about the significance of these features, it seems beyond reasonable doubt that there was a clear intention to present Nero "like" rather than "as" a god.

The death of Nero, hated as a tyrant for his cruelty and excesses, brought a reaction and at least a partial restoration of ideals of the Republic. This can be seen most clearly in the reverse designs discussed below, but also explains the reversion to the rugged style of portraiture, characteristic of Republican Rome (**45**). One can easily compare the general aspect of portraits of Galba (**86**), Vitellius or Vespasian (**87**) with the few ancestor portraits occurring on Republican coins of the mid first century BC. This reaction did not, however, outlast the accession of Domitian (AD 81–96) (**88**), who was in many respects like Nero, and indeed their iconography shows many similarities. Domitian abandoned the neo-Republican tradition, and returned to the Neronian type of portrait, together with its use of divine symbols, particularly the aegis, and again the same problem of interpretation arises for Domitian as for Nero. Does the aegis merely show that Domitian presented himself as under the divine protection of his favourite deity, Minerva? Or is it intended to indicate that he was, at least in some respects, like a god, as contemporary poets suggested?

In the early second century Trajan introduced as a standard variant the portrait of the emperor as a hero: bare shoulders and chest with only a cloak flung around (**90**). His successor Hadrian introduced the imperial fashion of wearing a beard (**92–3**), presumably in his case, as in that of Nero, as the mark of a philhellene. In similar ways, later emperors used their appearance and official portrait to express their ideals or aspirations. Marcus Aurelius adopted the long philosopher's beard (**98**), as a visible sign of his adherence to Stoic philosophy. His portrait was followed by those who wished to stress descent, whether real or imaginary, from this best of emperors: his son Commodus (**100**), Septimius Severus (**101**) and Macrinus, who "cultivated his beard", by changing his short beard to a long one, to stress his connexion with Marcus (Herodian 5.2.4).

Commodus was also the first emperor to use systematically the iconography of Hercules, with whom he apparently identified himself. Earlier emperors had occasionally borrowed from Hercules' iconography, in a long line going back to Mark Antony, but of these only Hadrian had left a few rare representations of himself as such on coins. Commodus, on the other hand, at the very end of his reign showed himself wearing the lion skin head-dress of Hercules (**100**). In using his portrait to stress a close connection with a particular deity he was followed by Septimius Severus, whose corkscrew curls were in imitation of Sarapis (**101**). The curious 'horn' shown on the last issues of Elagabalus must presumably also have some connection with his preferred cult, that of the sacred stone or Elagabal of Emisa in Syria, although the exact significance of the horn is elusive. This use of divine attributes became increasingly important in imperial portraiture during the third century, although the 'military' emperors of the first part preferred to show themselves without divine overtones, for example, Trajan Decius (**114**). Only with Gallienus, and Postumus (**121**) his rival in Gaul, did the association with Hercules revive, and thereafter was to be a very important part of the iconography of the pre-Christian emperors of late antiquity.

The designs used on the reverses of the coins also developed considerably. The Augustan coinage, as has been described, tended to have images of actual events, and referred directly to particular events. This was supplemented by the appearance of Roman gods and goddesses to whose favour the emperor owed his successes, for example, Apollo at Actium. Deities came to be a normal feature of the coinage, often reflecting the particular interest of a given emperor, like Domitian and Minerva, or Septimius Severus with Dionysus and Hercules, the patron deities of his birthplace. From the end of the reign of Augustus, however, gods and actual events or objects were supplemented with the more symbolic language of personifications. These had been extensively used in the Republic and came to play an equally important part in the repertoire of imperial designs, giving the rather curious characteristic of Roman coinage with its odd mixture of the concrete, the divine and the symbolic. The juxtaposition of the different elements can seem most awkward in a reign such as that of Claudius. On his coinage, flat statements of fact, for example the German or British victories (73), accompany highly obscure personifications like his idiosyncratic representations of Pax or Constantia, whose exact point is not clear to us, and presumably have some unknown complicated personal connection with the emperor.

The personifications have misleadingly been called "imperial virtues". But these figures, like Pietas, Providentia, Pudicitia, or Honos, did not represent a set of virtues canonical for a ruler, nor were they virtues in the sense accepted by ancient philosophers. They were rather qualities which an emperor might display or wish to be associated with his person. This can be seen most clearly in the link between the first appearance of a particular quality on the coinage and the adoption of that same quality by an emperor. For instance, Providentia first appears for Trajan (89), the first emperor to be referred to as *providentissimus*, while Commodus, the first emperor to be called *nobilissimus*, was the first to use Nobilitas on his coinage.

Sometimes these personifications could be used in a very specific way, and allude to some particular aspect, act or policy of an emperor. For example, Spes (Hope) appears on the coinage of Claudius, not because he wished to present his reign as offering promise for the future, but simply because he was born on August 1, the festival of Spes. Salus (safety) may appear on the occasion of an imperial journey, when vows were made "for the safety of the emperor". Salus also appears on the coinage of Commodus in AD 185 after the suppression of the plot of Perennis in that year; so do Concordia (*militum*, of the soldiers who had remained loyal) and Felicitas (Success).

There was a proliferation in the second century of the use of such personifications at the expense of the more concrete sort of design. Whereas the use of personifications had been sparing in the first century, even in the Flavian period, it later became very common, particularly from the reigns of Hadrian and Antoninus Pius onwards. This sudden upsurge in the use of personifications has been compared with contemporary literature. A glance through the first few pages of Pliny's *Panegyric* of Trajan, for instance, reveals a considerable interest in and reference to qualities, and similarly Suetonius's *Biographies* of the earlier Roman emperors, published in the reign of Hadrian, consistently judged its subjects by their good and bad qualities. In the same way, the coinage dwelt on the abstractions of the emperor's qualities, and displayed them in personified form.

The increasing use of personifications resulted in them becoming banal in time, particularly as there was little attempt at innovation. This shift is illustrated clearly by the celebration of *donatives* or presents of money from the emperor. At first these had been marked by the depiction of an actual scene of the emperor distributing coins, (**98** of Marcus Aurelius), but later all such scenes were replaced by the representation of the personification of Liberalitas (**109** of Severus Alexander). The effect of this emphasis on personifications and the repetition, from reign to reign, of similar personifications without (one suspects) the same specific references as before, was to render them increasingly meaningless. Little wonder that modern commentators have found so little of interest in them; what is more surprising is that there seems to have been a corresponding decline in interest at the time. A good example can be found in the civil wars of AD 193–7, where the contrast with the strident and explicit coin designs in the two previous civil wars (44–31 BC, and AD 68–69) could not be clearer. The designs used by Didius Julianus or by Pescennius Niger, for instance, would pass unnoticed among the gallery of types used by an emperor in a period of peace.

The entire language of coin design had thus become conventionalised. This change seems to be at least partly connected with the increasing rôle of the coin's design as the method of keeping a check on the output of the different sections in the mint. Since there was a strict relationship between each of the six sections and a particular design, the specific content of that design was bound to lose its primary rôle, and there would inevitably be a reluctance to innovate or change the designs. The need to produce exactly the same number of designs on each occasion that any change was required aggravated this tendency. The joint emperors Trebonianus Gallus and Volusian (251–3), for example, produced an issue comprising Felicitas, Libertas, Pietas, Concordia, Pax and Virtus: these may indicate the promise of a peaceful and militarily successful reign under the harmonious rule of two co-emperors, but are hardly very expressive or eye-catching, despite the chaotic history of the times. As with modern political jargon, constant repetition of abstractions and symbols had rendered them almost meaningless.

Designs on provincial coins

When we turn, however, to the designs used on the coins made in the provinces, we find a very different picture. Indeed the trend is almost a mirror image, from the bland to the particular, of what happens to the official coinage from Rome. During the period of the Republic, there was very little Romanisation of the traditional designs, as we saw in chapter three. The vast majority of issues, whether of silver or bronze, and whether of city, league or tribe, continued to use their own local and unchanging designs, generally with the head of a deity on the front and a complementary design on the back – usually another deity, or a symbol of a deity. The exceptions were few indeed before the imperial period, occurring only on the bronze coinage of Bithynia (**41**), to some extent on the silver coinages of the provinces of Asia and Syria, where the proconsul's name was added either in full or as a monogram (**42–3**), or on a rare tetradrachm of Gortyn, which commemorates the conquest of the island of Crete between 69 and 63 BC by Metellus Creticus. A head specifically labelled as the goddess Roma occurred on Spartan coinage during the first century BC; one may suspect that some of the "Athena/Minerva" heads elsewhere were supposed to be heads of the same goddess, but, if so, they were probably few in number (an interpretation as Athena is often more likely).

The civil wars of the late Republic brought some change, but less than one might have expected. Despite the widespread minting and circulation of denarii with the portraits and slogans of the different factions, these were not taken up on the civic coinage. Only occasionally, for instance on the coinage of Byzantium (**53**), do we encounter the person of Mark Antony; moreover, most of his portraits appear on coins struck by Cleopatra in her new Syrian possessions, where the recent change in regime might in any case have led one to expect some change. Elsewhere, there is very little; the same was true of the other leaders. Portraits occur only occasionally, for instance on the coinage of Sparta where Antony's general Atratinus and Octavian's admiral Agrippa appear on different occasions. Octavian's portrait is equally rare during the period of the civil war, appearing only on a few issues made in northern Italy (**48**) and Gaul (*see* chapter three). The reverse designs were even less affected than the obverse; and apart from an exceptional case like Byzantium, where the portrait of Antony was accompanied by a trophy referring to naval victory, even the cities which adopted a portrait continued to use local designs for the reverse.

With the establishment of sole rule by Augustus, all of this changed. Though the content of the reverses remained little altered, there was a dramatic increase in the appearance of the emperor's head, for example, (**66**) from Laodicea in Asia. In all, some two hundred communities throughout the Roman world issued coins with his portrait (Fig 3.2). This was a complete break with what had gone before, and it is extremely frustrating that we cannot date the appearance of these portraits at all accurately within the reign. Consequently we cannot assess whether this general adoption of the portrait was the spontaneous response of the cities to Augustus's position or whether it was officially orchestrated. The idea of central imposition may be unfashionable, but had apparently occurred in the kingdom of Syria in the second century BC, when the Seleucid king Antiochus IV had made all the cities in his kingdom put his portrait on their coins, as can be seen from the fact that these coins – which conveniently for us are dated – were minted from almost exactly the same year.

Syrian coins continued to bear dates in the imperial period, so we can date the arrival of the portrait fairly accurately there. It took place surprisingly late, in the last decade of the first century BC, probably rather later than elsewhere in the empire, as far as we can tell. Even so, its interpretation is unclear. The adoption of the portrait there seems to coincide more or less with the reform of the Roman provincial silver and bronze coinage from Antioch in 5 BC; the main element of the reform was the replacement of the old designs, a posthumous portrait of king Philip of Syria and a figure of Zeus (**43**), with the head of the emperor. But are we to suppose that the Syrian cities followed suit because they were told to do so by Quinctilius Varus (Augustus's legate, who introduced the reform), or because they saw the change at Antioch and naturally responded in the same way?

When we turn to consider the details of the portrait, matters are no clearer, both from the point of view of its general appearance and of the details of its transmission. One of the most noticeable general features of the civic portraits of Augustus is the almost universal reluctance of the cities to liken him to a god, whether by the use of divine symbols or by the inscription *theos*, "god". This reluctance is all the more striking when we compare it with the cities' treatment of the female members of Augustus's family, who are not infrequently likened to goddesses, or with their attitude to the cult of the emperor himself; more priests of Augustus are known than of any other emperor. Instead the cities portrayed him as a man, with an unadorned portrait head; the only symbol to occur at all regularly was the *lituus* or augur's crook (**66**), and its presence suggests that the Greek cities were aware of the Latin wordplay augur-Augustus, which according to Suetonius was one of the reasons for the choice of the new name. Yet, just as with the adoption of the portrait itself, it is not clear how we should interpret this mode of representation. Was it centrally directed? Not necessarily so. The idea of avoiding divine representations could easily have been picked up from the coinage of Rome, or indeed from any of the other popular arts of the period, while the portrayal of the emperor as augur might have been prompted by the many statues showing the emperor in a religious manner, with a veiled head, which were perhaps intended to show him as an augur.

A similar obscurity hangs over the question of the dissemination of the portrait itself throughout the cities who placed it on their coinage. We know from the sculptural portraits of Augustus that the imperial image was widely disseminated and that its realisations in the provinces adhered closely to a central pattern. This was no doubt the result of sending out patterns like the one we hear of in the inscription from Termessus in Asia, which records how a show was held in the amphitheatre "on the day that the sacred image of our lord Valerian, the new emperor, was brought" (*ILS* 8870, AD 253). Thus, it seems clear that an 'official' portrait would have been widely available, but it is remarkable in view of this that the treatment of the portrait on coins differs so widely in appearance and quality in the different cities. Sometimes the occurrence of stylistically very close representations of an emperor at nearby cities makes it clear that all are the work of a single engraver, who perhaps travelled from city to city, and that therefore they represent his interpretation; the same is even more true of the later period, when the 'shared workshop' system (*see* chapter two) was in operation. Sometimes it seems clear that other coins were copied, often imperial silver; this is hardly surprising, since to make a profile portrait it is much easier to copy a two- rather than a three-dimensional prototype. Beyond this it is hard to say anything which is either generally true or has any certainty; the portrait always tended to resemble at least roughly the official portrait, although as a result in a period like the first century AD when portraits were closely modelled on one of a predecessor we are often very unsure even which emperor is involved. This perhaps should not surprise us too much, as we know that in other art forms poor likenesses could be produced, for example, Arrian, on visiting Trapezus during the reign of Hadrian, wrote back to the emperor that "your statue is not like you and not at all attractive" (*Periplus* 1.3). Thus whatever the exact mechanisms for the dissemination of coin portraiture, it seems that there was no official system of regulation of the sort that is found, for instance, in the imperial mints of the late empire, but that each city or group of cities (or 'workshop') was reasonably free to produce its own images, which would for obvious reasons conform as far as possible to the official one.

Civic freedom, or rather the lack of any systematic control, may also be the partial explanation of one of the other somewhat surprising features of so many imperial provincial coins – that they have no imperial portrait at all. These coins, which have therefore misleadingly been called "pseudo-autonomous", were produced throughout the period and in large numbers, accounting perhaps for something like a quarter of the output of the cities (although this statistic is no more than a guess), and depict a whole range of subjects: gods, heroes, ancestors and personifications. Personifications, as with the imperial coinage, were particularly common from the second century, and we find many 'portraits' of the Roman senate, a city's *Demos* or "People", for example that of Tripolis in Asia (**97**) or one of its councils, for example the Gerousia or the Boule. But what historical importance are we to attach to these coins? Is there, or is there not, any significance in the absence of the emperor's portrait? There seems no satisfactory explanation for their existence in terms of the status of cities, as they occur at colonies, at free and at stipendiary cities, or in terms of denomination, although it is sometimes thought erroneously that the coins were all of small denominations, and so like the 'anonymous' semisses and quadrantes from second-century Rome (**96**). Nor can they be explained in terms of geographical location, for example the portrait of the Roman senate is common in the 'senatorial' province of Asia, but absent from the similarly 'senatorial' Bithynia. There were, however, some practical reasons for using them, since they allowed a particular denomination to be easily characterised, and since they will have been cheaper to produce, because the dies did not have to be changed at the beginning of each new reign. These advantages cannot, however, have been very important, or else this sort of coin would have been adopted everywhere. In fact some cities never produced them, for instance a prolific issuer like Ephesus. Perhaps we are creating a problem where none really exists. We do, indeed, know less about the control (if any) of civic designs than of their authorisation, but in the case referred to earlier, when Alexander

83

of Abonouteichos asked the emperor for permission for a coinage and its designs, the obverse design in question was not an imperial portrait, but the magic snake Glycon. Yet this particular aspect attracted no comment. Thus we should probably conclude that, despite an apparent lack of coherence with the concept of coinage as a symbol of sovereignty, the Romans found nothing surprising or notable about the appearance of civic coins without a portrait.

It has already been observed that the advent of empire and the imperial portrait had little effect on the reverse designs of the civic coinage, which continued to consist of local subjects such as patron deities, for example (**66**) has the local cult figure of the god Zeus. This is also true in a different way of the designs used by colonies of Roman citizens, as opposed to the Greek communities. Colonial designs appear, on the face of it, to have more topical references, for example, the statue of Augustus at Philippi (**76**), but this only reflects the fact that most of these communities had recently been founded, generally by Julius Caesar or Augustus himself, to settle veterans from the army, and that they were communities of Romans. To a colony of veterans recently settled at Philippi, a statue of Augustus would have had a similar signficance as a statue of a patron deity did for a Greek community founded centuries before: both represented their origins, in a purely local manner.

During the two and a half centuries that the coinage lasted, some trends in the designs uśed are naturally discernible. First of all, the designs used on the coinage came to share the antiquarian revival so evident in other art forms of the Roman provinces, which the coins sometimes copied, particularly from the second century AD. Personifications of imaginary founders, mythical and mythological scenes connected with the city's foundation or history come to abound, for example Leander swimming the Hellespont towards his lover Hero, on a coin of Commodus from Abydus (**99**), taking over from the more austere choices of patron deities, which had characterised the coinage of the first century. Again, just as the fewer designs used in the first century on the coinage of Rome proliferated in the second, so it was in the provinces; as well as scenes from local myth, depictions of actual objects appear more frequently, such as buildings, for example the gateway of Augusta Traiana on a coin of Caracalla (**102**), temples or bridges, such as that at Antioch in Asia on a coin of Gallienus (**117**). We also find actual events being shown, such as a meeting of the town council, for example Alexandria Troas (**115**) or a gladiatorial show, like that at Synnada (**118**). In many ways the designs used on imperial provincial coins came to resemble those used on Republican denarii. Both refer to events in the mythological or historical past, important buildings, and, as we shall see, contemporary events. This similarity stems from the similar use of designs. Republican moneyers wished to stress their origins or present connections to enhance their reputation, and so did the cities of the provinces: once again we should recall that the Sestos inscription gives civic pride as one of the motives for coinage, and we know that relative status was one of the most controversial issues between the cities of the empire.

This shift towards the depiction of the actual and of contemporary events is connected with the second interesting change in civic designs, namely the increasing frequency with which the emperor or his achievements was represented. Early in the empire such references were almost non-existent. In the reign of Augustus, for instance, there is almost only a solitary example, when the coinage of Apamea in Asia celebrated the expedition of Augustus's adoptive son Gaius to the east. The first rather more regular references to the emperor occur in the reign of Nero, when we find his visit to Greece in AD 66/7 celebrated on the coinage of several of the cities he visited, for example the coinage of Corinth marked his arrival by galley (84). From this period on, the number of topical references to the emperor increased, often in conjunction with an imperial visit, but also more generally: Trajan's Parthian victory, for instance, was recorded on the coinage of cities in Asia, for example, Ephesus (91) and Tripolis. The result of this tendency to multiply the variety of representations on civic coinage was that by the third century it contrasted curiously with that minted at Rome, where the variety of designs had been greatly diminished through the practice of having one type per section of the mint and through the increasing emphasis on conventional abstractions rather than concrete events. The civic coinage, as a result, continued to exhibit a quite different variety and vitality, for example a victory of the emperor Philip celebrated on the coinage of Bizya (111), and, as such, it continued to enhance the prestige of the city which issued it and the emperor whose rule it honoured. Yet it was the inability of these same emperors to balance the finances of the empire which led to the sudden cessation of this flourishing phenomenon.

Chapter Five

Circulation and function

Closed and open currency systems

In the ancient world there were basically two monetary systems, each of which required different sorts of regulation and protection. These two, which can be called the "closed" and the "open" monetary systems, were really only different ends of the same spectrum, and intermediate stages were also possible. The extreme form of closed system was to be found in the Ptolemaic and Pergamene kingdoms in Egypt and Asia respectively during the Hellenistic period. As described in chapter three, both of these closed systems remained intact when the areas were taken over by the Romans. These kingdoms allowed only a single coinage – in Egypt, Ptolemaic, and later Roman, tetradrachms; in Asia, the cistophori – so all foreigners had to change their money into the local currency. At the other end of the spectrum lay the open system, where all coins were in principle free to circulate. The example of fourth-century Athens, revealed by a recently published inscription, shows that although only Athenian coinage, defined as coin "which is silver and bears the official die (*character*)", was legally enforceable, foreign coins were also allowed in the city. In this example the state's own coinage would in fact have circulated at a small premium (a 5% overvaluation between the face value and the bullion value of the coin); since other coins were not legally enforceable, they would tend to be discounted down towards their bullion value.

Variations on these systems were also possible. For instance, a closed system might be accompanied by a coinage of large bronze coins with a relatively high face value, to try and ensure that most internal transactions took place in bronze, reserving precious metals for foreign trade; or a state might insist not only that just its own coins should be used, but also, as in Ptolemaic Egypt, that they must be unworn. Conversely, one supposes that the many small independent communities without their own coinage allowed all coins to circulate indiscriminately.

What sort of monetary system did the Roman government

impose? In the broadest sense it was a closed system, since the coins of foreign states, for example coins of Parthia or of Carthage, were not normally allowed to circulate, unless they happened to represent part of the circulating medium in an area taken over by the Romans and where the Romans made no change to that currency. Thus, for instance, late Ptolemaic tetradrachms continued to circulate in early Roman Egypt. But within the Roman world there were, as the survey in chapter three indicated, a large number of different sorts of coin – cistophori (**42, 50, 57** and **93**), Alexandrian tetradrachms (**69, 107–8** and **130**), Iberian denarii (**36**) and so on – and one naturally wonders how their circulation was regulated. In Egypt, as we have seen, the Romans maintained the strictly closed currency system of their Ptolemic predecessors for another three hundred years until the reform of Diocletian in about AD 296, and those transacting business in Egypt had to use the local silver and bronze coins. The only alteration to the Ptolemaic system was, presumably, that Roman gold could be freely brought in and used, as the hoards of gold discovered there suggest.

The same situation prevailed in Asia during the Republic, where the Romans took over the currency of the kingdom of Pergamum, which was based on the cistophorus, in 133 BC, just as they were to take over the Ptolemaic system a hundred years later. In Republican Syria, however, they took over the royal coinage of the Seleucid dynasty, but probably, like the Seleucids, did not insist on a monopoly of this currency. We may perhaps imagine a system in operation there similar to that of fourth-century Athens, with the Roman tetradrachms (**80**) perhaps enjoying a small premium in state transactions, although the situation was probably more complicated in view of the parallel circulation of the finer coins of Tyre (**77**). Thus in the late Republican period in Syria and Asia it looks as if the two different systems of the Hellenistic world were continued for a time. In both areas, however, from about the time of the civil wars (44–31 BC) and the reign of Augustus (31 BC–AD 14), Roman denarii also began to circulate. These denarii did not at first replace the cistophori or tetradrachms, which continued to be minted as well as to circulate, but the two sorts of money, denarius and local silver, circulated together. A similar situation had existed in Republican Spain in the second and first centuries BC, where Roman denarii and Iberian denarii both circulated, sometimes occurring together in hoards. In all these three cases, Syria, Spain and Asia, in contrast to Egypt, the denarius appears to have been universally acceptable, whereas the local coinages were not and did not leave their own area.

To a certain extent this localised circulation will have been encouraged by the intrinsic value of the coins, as normally coins with restricted circulation contained less silver than their equivalent in the denarius system, for example the cistophori of Asia apparently contained 25% less silver than their equivalent in denarii. This cannot have been the whole story, however, since on some rare occasions local coins contained more silver than their denarius equivalents. By contrast, the silver drachms minted by Trajan (AD 98–117) in Lycia (southern Turkey) also contained less silver than an equivalent denarius, yet they circulated widely outside Lycia, turning up, for instance, in British hoards in small but regular quantities. The mechanism for controlling the circulation area of local silver coinage must therefore have been more complex. In areas where local silver and denarii of greater intrinsic worth circulated together, there must anyway have been some legal compulsion to accept the two coins together, or else "bad" money would have driven out "good"; conversely, this legal compulsion could have defined the (greater or lesser) area where this artificially higher value was valid, thereby allowing a greater or lesser area of circulation for the coins in question.

Reasons for minting

The existence of these closed currency systems within the Roman world implies that at least some of their local coinages were minted for the purpose of satisfying the need of businessmen and other travellers to have the local currency for their transactions in the relevant areas. New coins would have to be minted regularly, partly so that the moneychangers would have an adequate supply to exchange with them (after all, the profit on such transactions was the whole point of the system), but also perhaps so that individual travellers arriving in the area could have their own coins melted down and re-minted into the local ones at the mint. This was, at any rate, what happened in the closed system of Ptolemaic Egypt, as we can see from a letter written in the third century BC by a man called Demetrios, perhaps the head of the Ptolemaic mint, to Apollonios, the finance minister of the kingdom:

"As for me, I am attending to the work as you wrote to me to do, and I have received in gold 57,000 pieces, which I minted and returned. We might have received many times as much, but as I wrote to you once before, the foreigners who come here by sea and the merchants and the middlemen and others bring their own pure coin and gold pentadrachms

PLATE 9

59

60

61

62

63

64

65

66

67

PLATE 10

68

69

70

71

72

73

74

75

76

PLATE 11

77

78

79

80

81

82

83

84

85

86

87

88

PLATE 12

89

90

91

92

93

94

95

96

97

PLATE 13

98

99

100   101

102   103   104

PLATE 14

105

106

107

108

109

110

111

112

113

PLATE 15

114

115

116

117

118

119

120

121

122

123

PLATE 16

124

125

126

128

127

129

130

131

to be made into new coin for them in accordance with the decree which orders us to receive and re-mint, but as Philetaerus [?] does not allow me to accept, not knowing to whom we can appeal on the subject, we are compelled not to accept [. . .]; and they complain because their gold is not accepted by the banks or by us for [. . .], nor are they able to send it into the country to buy goods, but their gold, they say, is lying idle and they are suffering no little loss, having sent for it from abroad and being unable to dispose of it easily to other persons even at a reduced price. Moreover, all the people in the city find it difficult to make use of their worn gold. For none of them knows to what authority he can refer and on paying something extra receive either good gold or silver in exchange. Now things being as they are, I see that the revenues of the king are also suffering no little harm. . . . I take it to be an advantage if as much gold as possible be imported from abroad and the king's coinage be always good and new without any expense falling on him" (*Select Papyri* II.409, 258 BC).

This letter throws fascinating light on the working of a closed currency system – and its potential problems – and it seems likely that something of the same machinery was in operation in Republican Asia and in Egypt to allow those travelling or transacting business there to obtain an adequate supply of the required coinage. This would therefore have provided an important reason for the regular minting of new coin in these areas.

A second reason would have been provided by the occasions on which the currency of all or part of the Roman world was changed by the government for some reason (whether economic or political). The resulting demonetisations will have prompted the production of much new coinage from the bullion so taken out of circulation; and this bullion will have been returned (at least in part!) to its former owners in the form of newly minted coin. Some examples of such recoinages were mentioned in chapter three. The most important affecting the denarius coinage were: the recoinage of the Hannibalic War, the recoinage of Trajan (after he withdrew most Republican denarii from circulation), and that of Trajan Decius (a major withdrawal of denarii in favour of radiates). There were of course other minor examples, such as the withdrawal of early imperial denarii, perhaps by Nerva (AD 96–98), or of the legionary denarii of Mark Antony by Marcus Aurelius and Lucius Verus (AD 161–169). Similar withdrawals and recoinages affected the local silver coinages, for example the withdrawal of Ptolemaic tetradrachms by Nero and his subsequent massive issues of silver from Alexandria, or Hadrian's recoinage of cistophori of Antony, Augustus and Claudius in Asia Minor.

The nature of closed currency systems and of recoinages can thus provide a motive for the minting of some new coinage in the Roman world, but it is unlikely that overall they provided such an important reason as the needs of state expenditure, pre-eminent amongst which seems to have been the need to meet military expenditure. We can see this from the particularly large issues of coinage that were minted during the periods of war like the Social War of 91–88 BC (*see* Fig. 5.1) or the civil wars of the late Republic, or from a comparison with pre-industrial modern Europe, for instance in the sixteenth century, where it has been estimated that 65–70% of all state revenues were spent on war. Likewise the historian and senator Dio could have Agrippa say: "our present revenues are insufficient to provide for the army and everything else" (52.6.1), thereby implying that the cost of the army was thought to be the biggest single item in the state budget.

The rôle of the denarius in military spending will have become particularly important from the middle of the second century BC, since it seems likely that the change which took place at about that time from a predominantly bronze coinage to a predominantly silver one indicates a shift in the medium of military pay from bronze to silver. From that date on it has been argued that there is a close correlation between the size of different issues of denarii with the number of soldiers in the Roman army at any given time. This correlation is based on a fairly straightforward, but much debated, statistical methodology. The first stage is to establish the number of dies used to produce a sample of coins (normally those represented in museum collections or a group of hoards). By examining each coin individually, one can tell which were struck from the same die and thus count the number of dies which were used to make them. If it is known how many dies were represented in this sample and in what proportion, probability theory can be used to estimate the total number of dies for the whole issue. Suppose, for instance, a sample of 1000 passing cars was observed on a street corner. If 127 were Fiats, 87 Vauxhalls, 32 Fords and so on, then the total number of different sorts of car on the road could be estimated reasonably accurately.

Secondly, one can then give a value to the average output of each die, using the rare cases in the ancient world when we know from external historical or epigraphic sources how many coins were minted in a particular issue whose dies we can count. The relevant data are rather uncertain, but an average output of between 30,000 and 50,000 coins seems to be the most likely, although this is much disputed, and lower figures such as 10,000 to 15,000 are sometimes preferred. Finally, as it is obviously rather impracticable to count the numbers of dies in this way for every single denarius issue, the procedure which has been adopted is to count a few sample issues and hence estimate the probable total of dies used for them, and then to extrapolate the probable number of dies used for other issues, based on the relative frequency of those other issues in hoards as compared with the sample issues. This is possible since their representation in hoards enables us to gauge the relative size of different issues; it has been shown for the modern period that there is a fairly close relationship between the number of coins in a given year represented in a hoard and the number of coins known from documentary sources to have been minted in that year.

Needless to say, there are all sorts of difficulties with this method. How certain is the correlation between representation in hoards and mint output? How accurate is the application of probability theory to estimate the total number of dies? What accuracy should be claimed for the average output in individual cases, in view of the medieval evidence which shows a wide variation in average output, even when the total number of dies is very large? And, most seriously, how sure are we of the average output per die? These are all more or less problematical, and the difficulties should not be underestimated, since if the limits of accuracy in the whole procedure are too wide, then the procedure itself loses its value. However, the current consensus seems to be that while there are real problems in defining the limits of accuracy, they are not hopeless, and that therefore the procedure is worthwhile, provided it is recognised that it can give only an approximation. It can be used only to indicate the general order of magnitude of a coin issue, and can certainly not be used to make anything like detailed calculations or comparisons.

In the particular case of the proposed correlation between numbers of denarii produced and the cost of the Roman army, one can avoid some of these practical difficulties (particularly the special uncertainty of absolute figures) by using only the final part of the procedure, that is to say, by examining the correlation between the size of the army and the representation of individual issues in the hoards, as this should provide a more accurate, if only relative, check on the correlation between the two. If one does this, then one finds that there is some correlation, but that it is not in fact very close (*see* Fig. 5.1). Periods of high expenditure, i.e. when there were a lot of legions in the army, correspond to large issues of coins, but little more. Moreover,

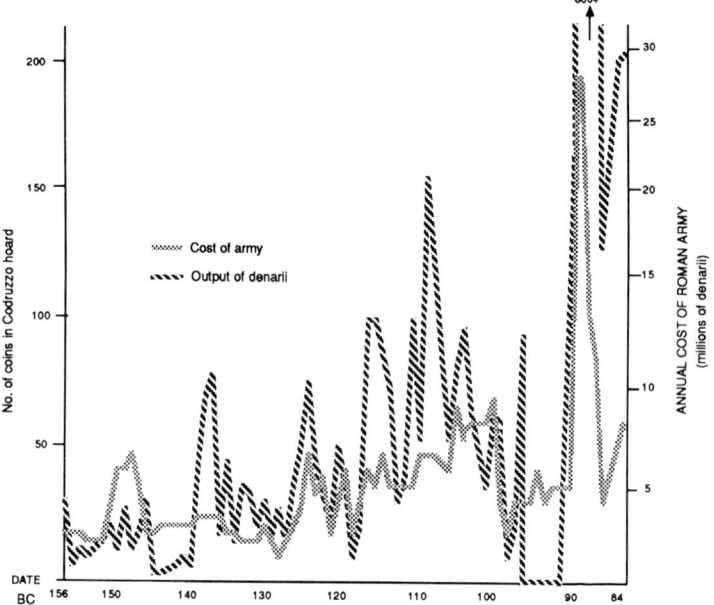

FIG. 5.1 *Relative Output and the Cost of the Republican Army*
A comparison between the number of coins in the large Monte Codruzzo hoard and the approximate cost of the Roman army between 156 and 84 BC shows only a very approximate correlation.

the theory of close correlation involves two rather unlikely assumptions; firstly that all soldiers were paid in denarii rather than local silver as well (which was minted on a large scale in the Republic, as described in chapter three), and, secondly, that they were paid solely in newly minted coin. The recirculation of old coin seems more likely, supplemented with annual additions of new coin. This certainly seems to have been the case in the imperial period, as we can see both from a specific example of a coin hoard probably contained in the official container in which it left the treasury (the hoard from Lay in France), and from the general pattern of coin issue, which fluctuates widely despite the existence of a static army of a fairly stable size. For instance, virtually no denarii at all were minted for some thirty years from the end of Tiberius's reign until AD 64. Again, if we look at the detailed pattern of minting under Domitian, for instance, we can see a substantial fluctuation from year to year (Fig. 5.2). These fluctuations cannot be explained even in terms of greater spending on, for example, equipment in wartime, since periods of war do not coincide with periods of high minting, and therefore other items of expenditure, such as retirement payments to soldiers, donatives and the cost of public buildings or roads, must also be taken into consideration.

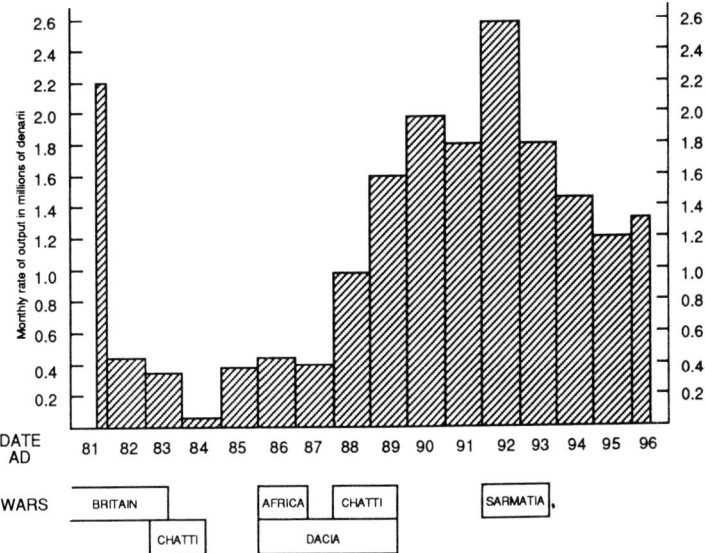

FIG. *5.2 Coinage and Wars under Domitian (AD 81–96)*
The output of denarii did not correspond to periods of warfare. (After I.
Carradice Coinage and Finances in the Reign of Domitian, *91.*)

Coinage in the state budget

If it is accepted that old coin was recirculated, then it becomes theoretically quite impossible to work out exactly how much the Roman state spent in any given year, since this can no longer be defined in terms of the quantity of coinage minted in that year. The attempt to estimate the size of the Roman state budget should therefore shift away from the particular to the more general, since individual annual changes can no longer be detected, and it should also concentrate more on other sorts of evidence than the coins themselves. One can discover a certain amount about the scale of various sorts of expenditure from literature and inscriptions, as indeed one can from comparative evidence from other, better documented, pre-industrial societies. Using this information, one can construct a flow diagram (Fig. 5.3) of the circulation of coin within the Roman state budget, for an average year in the early empire (the figures are in denarii and are very approximate).

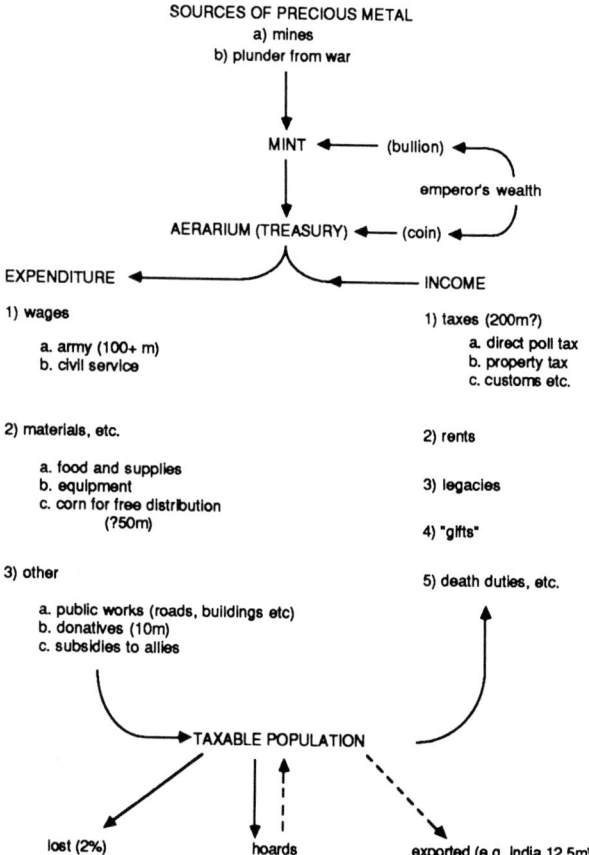

SOURCES OF PRECIOUS METAL
a) mines
b) plunder from war

MINT ◄——— (bullion) ◄

emperor's wealth

AERARIUM (TREASURY) ◄——— (coin) ◄

EXPENDITURE ◄

INCOME

1) wages

a. army (100+ m)
b. civil service

1) taxes (200m?)

a. direct poll tax
b. property tax
c. customs etc.

2) materials, etc.

a. food and supplies
b. equipment
c. corn for free distribution
(?50m)

2) rents

3) legacies

4) "gifts"

3) other

a. public works (roads, buildings etc)
b. donatives (10m)
c. subsidies to allies

5) death duties, etc.

TAXABLE POPULATION

lost (2%)   hoards   exported (e.g. India 12.5m)

FIG. 5.3 *The Circulation of Coin within the Roman State Budget*

This diagram naturally represents considerable oversimplifications; for instance the "Treasury" is here an amalgam of three elements: the traditional state treasury, the *aerarium militare* or military pension fund, and the *fiscus* or emperor's personal funds. However, in practice the distinction between these was often blurred, particularly that between the treasury and the *fiscus*: as Dio wrote, "nominally public funds were separated from his own [the emperor's], but in fact he spent them as he wished" (53.16.1). Equally significant were the emperor's subventions to the public treasuries, since his personal fortune was relatively so large that it played an essential part in the financial system of the empire, representing a substantial part of the state's resources. Augustus, for instance, gave 37.5 million denarii to the *aerarium* and 42 million to the *aerarium militare*, which was normally financed from a 5% death duty and a sales tax (?at an annual rate of 75 million).

Some of the figures in the diagram are naturally rather more hard to establish than others. For instance, we can be fairly confident of the annual cost of the imperial army, since we know roughly how large it was and how much each soldier was paid (225 denarii a year, rising to 300 denarii from AD 84/5.) The figure given to the revenue from direct taxation, however, is much more approximate since it is based on estimates of the size of the population, its minimum gross product (the cash value of its subsistence needs) and the likely level of taxation (10%). Even so, it seems reasonable to think that the diagram will indicate the scale of magnitude of the Roman state budget. In this respect it is a great shame that the *rationes imperii*, accounts for the empire, which Augustus kept and which were published after his death (Suetonius, *Augustus* 101) and whose regular annual publication was temporarily revived by Gaius (Suetonius, *Gaius* 16), have not survived. It looks, however, as if the annual budget amounted to something like 300 million denarii. This puts the size of new issues of coin into some sort of perspective; although the production of coin was rather irregular in the first century AD, in a reign of fairly substantial coining like that of Domitian (AD 81–96) it has been estimated that the annual production of denarii never exceeded 33 million, and was usually much lower (an average of 15 million).

Coinage in everyday life

These statistics, crude though they may be, give us some indication of the extent of coin circulation in terms of the state budget of the empire, but they give little idea of its rôle and function as far as the average inhabitant of the Roman world was concerned. It was suggested in chapter one that, during the third century BC, coinage played only a restricted part both in the finances of the state and in the day-to-day life of ordinary people, but this position seems to have changed with the huge increase in the amount of coinage produced from about 200 BC. From that time there was a full range of denominations small enough to be useful for the everyday needs of retail trading. For the Republican period, for instance, modern finds reveal the following pattern:

	Site		
denomination	Minturnae	River Liri	Cosa
as	17	154	118
semis	8	11	14
triens	8	44	15
quadrans	8	57	36
sextans	6	80	7

During this period the two staple foods of the ancient world, bread and wine, cost about a semis for a loaf, and about an as for a litre of ordinary wine, so we can see that the range of denominations would have been sufficient for everyday use in urban areas. The finds from the river Liri represent the good luck charms thrown into the river at a crossing, and hence show a bias towards the smaller denominations. More important is the fact that they demonstrate that coins were carried by people in the country, as well as in the cities. We know this too from Polybius's reference to people using coins at country inns (II.15.6), but the excavation of rural sites, such as Roman villas, has revealed a dearth of coins. We should presumably interpret this absence as showing that, although coins were carried in the country by people travelling through it, they were not normally used to any very large extent by the rural population. This is perhaps what we should expect, given the different and less specialised nature of ancient farming, where there would be less need to purchase everyday items.

In contrast to the countryside, excavated urban sites have revealed large numbers of coins; the excavations in the Roman Forum, for instance, have brought many thousands of coins to light, and they show a similar range of convenient small denominations. The face value of these small demoninations gradually increased over the years, as a result of the debasement of the precious metal coinage and the consequent rise of prices (*see* chapter six). They did, however, continue to maintain a sufficiently wide range of denominations for retail trade, except perhaps in the northern provinces of the empire, where there seems to have been a shortage of the smaller denominations (such as the semis and the quadrans in the early first century) in comparison to the cities of the Mediterranean, perhaps implying a more restricted use of coin in small transactions.

The widespread use of coinage for everyday transactions in towns and villages can be vividly illustrated by Apuleius's novel *The Golden Ass* or, for Egypt, by surviving papyri. These papyri demonstrate a full use of coined money, even in villages and for the simplest transactions. One such papyrus from Oxyrhynchus (*POxy* 736 = Select Papyri 1.186) details the everyday accounts of some individual in the early imperial period (the figures are given in drachmae consisting of 6 obols; there were 4 drachmae to the denarius):

22nd	1 measure of oil 4dr 4ob
	wax and stylus for the children 1 ob
	pure bread for Prima ½ ob
	for entertaining Tyche 3 ob
17th	milk for the children ½ ob
	pure bread ½ ob
18th	to Secundus for a cake for the children ½ ob
19th	barley water for the same ½ ob
21st	pomegranates for the children 1 ob
	toys for the children ½ ob
	beer 3 ob
	sauce 1 ob

Problems of liquidity

While the range of denominations seems to have been generally adequate for the Romans to have lived in a monetary economy, it is still necessary to see whether the total number of coins was sufficient to meet demand. The evidence seems to show that, in general, the supply of money was normally sufficient, but that on fairly frequent occasions it was not and prompted a crisis of liquidity, whereby a shortage of actual coin caused real problems, sometimes quite severe. The most obvious instances are indicated by the large-scale production of 'copies' or 'forgeries' of bronze coins, of which there were two particular periods, in the first century BC (**49**), and in the middle of the first century AD (**75**), when copies were produced in huge numbers all over the western part of the Roman world (*see* chapter three). In some northern areas such as Britain they greatly outnumbered official coins, but they also occurred in substantial numbers in areas such as Italy.

Although a shortage of bronze coins would have been inconvenient, shortages of silver had potentially far more serious consequences. In the first centuries BC and AD, we hear of a surprising number of such crises of liquidity, surprising because they took place in a period when extremely large numbers of coins were being produced, all of which must have gone straight out of circulation and into hoards. Such shortages occurred in 63, 49, 44, perhaps 7, BC and AD 33, and in some of these instances we hear of a "shortage of coins" (*nummorum caritas*: Cicero, *Letters to Atticus* 9.9.4, 49 BC).

The consequences of these shortages were partly economic, inasmuch as they pushed up the prices of gold and land, if not of other items. But there were also serious social consequences. Those who could not meet their debts were threatened with having to sell their property on a rapidly falling market, and, at least in 7 BC, this led to riots, while in 63 BC the shortage of liquidity may have exacerbated the debt problem and contributed to the causes of Catiline's insurrection. Although force was always used to put down riot or rebellion, the responses of the Republic and imperial governments were otherwise rather different. In the Republic the only measures taken were attempts, no doubt ineffective, to increase liquidity by banning the export of money (63 BC) or the hoarding of sums greater than 15,000 denarii (49 BC), whereas in the imperial period the emperor solved the problem by making large interest-free loans available, presumably in the form of cash: Augustus lent 15 million denarii from 7 BC, and Tiberius 25 million in AD 33.

It may reasonably be pointed out that crises of this kind probably affected mainly the richer, propertied, strata of Roman society, and that the temporary rise in prices caused by such shortages did not include the smaller items of retail trade, whose prices were affected more by seasonal variation and long term trends in the amount of money in circulation (*see* chapter six). Consequently, the poorer members of Roman society would not have been much harmed by these short-term problems.

Ordinary people did, however, need the protection of the state in other ways, as we can see from the crisis (whose exact nature eludes us) of 86 or 85 BC, when, in Cicero's words, "the coinage was being so tossed about that no one could tell what he had" (*iactabatur enim temporibus illis nummus sic, ut nemo posset scire quid haberet*: *de Officiis* 3.20.80). We do not know what solution was found by the praetor Gratidianus, but it prompted an extraordinary popular reaction. Statues were set up to him at every street corner, and incense and candles were offered at them, as if he were a god. "No one was ever dearer to the multitude", adds Cicero, and even allowing for exaggeration, the story makes it clear how important a stable coinage was to the Roman populace at large. It was not merely a matter of minor interest to a small part of Roman society.

The causes of this crisis have been variously explained, in

terms of plated forgeries, debasement of the coinage, a shortage of coin or a volatile exchange rate between silver and bronze coins. Whatever the exact cause in this case, however, it seems that some at least of these suggested explanations did provide problems which regularly beset the smooth functioning of the coinage for ordinary people, and hence required official intervention from time to time.

Forgery and abuse

The two main areas where official protection was required were in ensuring that the coinage was properly produced and that once produced it was not the object of abuse or malpractice. The attempts to ensure that adequate controls operated in the mint have already been mentioned in chapter two, in particular the use of "control-marks" on Republican denarii (**27**) in the first half of the first century BC. We have little detailed information about the malpractices of mint-workers, who presumably had the opportunity to forge coins within the mint and to steal genuine ones. Such dishonesty was so embedded that in the fourth century it could be suggested that mints should be situated on islands and their workers should be denied all access to the outside world (Anon., *de rebus bellicis* 3.1–3)! Moreover, the likely interpretation of the apparent existence of genuine silver and silver-plated coins struck from the same die is that they do not represent "official" attempts to issue plated coins alongside genuine ones, but that they represent forgeries made with official dies, probably outside the mint. The theft of dies is implied by the legislation against it (*Dig.* 48.13.8), while in the late empire, people who allowed their houses to be used for counterfeiting by moneyers were banished and had their property confiscated (*CTh* 9.21.2). It seems not improbable that the two genuine dies for Augustan silver and gold coins, which were found in 1789 during excavations in the fountain of Diana at Nimes in France (a most unlikely place for a mint) had been stolen in this way.

Plated coins – of base metal with a surface plating of fine silver – could be produced by a variety of methods. One method, the so-called "cliché" method, also has a bearing on the phenomenon of die sharing between plated and genuine coins. In this procedure, a genuine coin was taken and placed on a thin sheet of silver on top of a piece of lead. It was then hammered into the soft lead, producing a perfect impression in the silver foil. The same was done for the reverse, and the two pieces of foil were then soldered together and filled up with base metal. The resulting forgery would appear to have been made from the same genuine die as its model. Another method consisted of casting coins in clay moulds, made by impressing genuine coins in them. Many such moulds, and indeed some of the workshops which produced them and base metal casts from them, have been found in northern Europe: these mostly date from the early third century AD. Although it has been suggested that these moulds were used to produce bronze coins, because penalties for forging bronze were less severe, it seems more likely that the base metal cores were subsequently plated with silver, since it seems odd that a forger of bronze coins should choose silver rather than bronze coins as the models for his forgeries.

One cannot overestimate the scale of the problem that plated forgeries posed to the smooth circulation of coin, as throughout the period these seem to have been the most serious type of forgery. Although plated coins are indeed rare in hoards, they are nevertheless very commonly found in excavations; approximately one half of all denarii found on a site tend to be plated. Obviously site finds are biased towards objects of low value, just as hoards are biased in the opposite direction, but it is still clear that they must have existed in substantial numbers for so many to be available, even if only for discarding. How was the problem dealt with? In Republican times it may have prompted the mint to produce coins with notched or serrate edges (**30**), which look as if they would be harder to make as plated coins. This was, however, not so, as the large numbers of plated serrate coins show, but it might have helped inspire some confidence: Tacitus records that the Germans, living beyond the frontier, preferred "serrati" (*Germ.* 5.5). A more effective response to the problem can be seen in the role of the *nummularii* (bankers or testers) who inspected coins for plating and often stamped them with little punch marks, sometimes in the form of a letter, for example the small x on the emperor's neck (**56**), to check their quality. Checked coins were put in bags and sealed with tags sometimes made of ivory, which survive today (**35**, of 76 BC). These nummularii are attested not just from Rome, but also from other cities throughout Italy; they no doubt also existed outside Italy, although coins from Spain apparently almost always lack punch marks. The earliest of these tags is dated to 96 BC, and the practice of punching continued throughout the first century BC until the reign of Augustus, when it was discontinued, perhaps out of deference to the emperor's image.

Other forgeries were produced in different ways. They might be cast from genuine coins or struck from false dies. The first sort of forgery is comparatively rare in the Roman world; apart from the Severan "denarii" already discussed, the only noticeable cases are the lightweight casts of asses, typical of the Rhineland provinces in the early third century AD (the so-called "limesfalsa"), or a small but definite percentage of the false radiates made at the end of the century (*see* chapter seven). Struck forgeries were more common, and coins (including plated ones) were made in this way in all metals, although comparatively rarely in the case of gold and silver. Usually such precious metal forgeries were made outside the empire: gold was copied in India in the Severan period, and silver in Romania during the Republic (from dies manufactured so cleverly from genuine coins that their products are sometimes virtually indetectable). The majority of these forgeries were, however, the bronze imitations of the late Republic and early empire, which have already been described; similar "epidemics" of such forgery afflicted the late empire (*see* chapter seven).

The attitude of the state towards these forgeries seems, rather surprisingly to our way of thinking, to have varied according to the intrinsic value of the forgery and the status of the forger. We tend to associate the idea of forgery with treason, since tampering with the sovereign's "image and superscription" can be construed as such. This attitude was also certainly possible in antiquity. It is of course implicit in the link between coinage and sovereignty (*see* chapter two), and in the fourth century it could be explicitly stated that counterfeiting "reduces the image of royal majesty" (*regiae maiestatis imaginem imminuit*: Anon., *de rebus bellicis* 2.1). This attitude was certainly applied to the forging of gold coin. Those tampering with gold were condemned to the beasts, if they were freeborn, or executed, if they were slaves (*Dig.* 48.10.9), but the penalty for forgery of silver was less severe: for the freeborn, for instance, only exile (Paul, *Sententiae* 5.25.1). Most surprising of all, however, is the apparent absence in Roman law of any provision for dealing with the forging of bronze; at any rate nothing has survived among the fairly scanty information we have. This absence may partly be fortuitous, inasmuch as the first systematic body of forgery legislation, the *lex Cornelia de falsis*, was drawn up by Sulla at a time when bronze coinage was not being produced and so it might not have been thought necessary to include any measures dealing with it. Even so, the absence of any surviving provisions seems somewhat surprising, although it can hardly be believed that the practice of forging bronze was not illegal.

The moneychangers

The second major area of potential hindrance in the smooth functioning of the coinage lay with the moneychangers, whose rôle in the circulation of coinage in antiquity was extremely important. Their rôle was twofold: to change foreign currency into local, and to change coins of one metal into coins of another. Both roles were important in the Roman world. The diversity of the coinage, particularly in silver, in use in different parts of the empire required a mechanism for its exchange. For instance, a soldier bringing back locally minted silver from Greece to Italy (as has been found in some hoards) would have to be able to change it into denarii before he could use it. Similarly, on arrival in Republican Asia or Ptolemaic Egypt, it would have been necessary to exchange one's coins for the cistophori or tetradrachms which circulated exclusively there. A commission (collybus) was charged on these exchanges, as it is by banks today. The profit made in this way, however, did not just benefit private corporations, since the moneychangers operated under official control and either purchased the right to their position or passed on their profits to the licensor (normally the city in which they operated). A commission was also charged on their other main activity, changing coins of one metal into those of another, and the profit made on such transactions was a constant source of aggravation. "The exchange commission for gold is quite bad enough," Cicero remarked in a letter, and sometimes complaints about the extortionate behaviour of the moneychangers were laid before the emperor. A good example occurred at Pergamum in the reign of Hadrian (AD 117–38), and Hadrian's judgement has been preserved in an inscription, which reveals the purpose of and complexities in the system:

"For although they [the bankers] were bound to accept 18 asses per denarius from the tradesmen, small stallholders and fishmongers, all of whom normally deal in small bronze, and to pay out 17 asses to those who wished to exchange a denarius, they were not satisfied with the exchange of asses, but even in cases where someone bought a fish for silver denarii they exacted an as for each denarius."

Complicated regulations then follow, which provided that small fishes must be paid for in bronze coin, unless they were priced in silver denarii, and that people could not get together in groups to pay for a lot of fish in silver, but had to pay in bronze at a rate of 17 asses per denarius, if their total purchase came to a denarius or more. The inscription then turns to other abuses:

Circulation and function

"They were then shown to have made agreements among themselves for other types of profit, namely unworn coin (*aspratoura*) and so-called kickbacks with which they abused particularly the fishmongers . . . and these therefore I also decided to correct" (*OGIS* 484).

Some of these abuses are easier to understand than others. Clearly the bankers had discounted against worn coin, by offering a lower rate, and this was simply banned. In the case of the fishmongers, the situation was more complicated and the emperor wanted to strike a balance between preventing the moneychangers from taking an excessive commission on the exchange of silver for bronze, while at the same time stopping individuals from evading payment of the due commission. His motives were twofold, fairness and the wish to preserve revenue: he acted "so that as a result the revenue from the commission (*ten ek tou collybou prosodon*) would be preserved for the city".

It comes as something of a surprise to see that although the denarius was officially tariffed at 16 asses (and official calculations were based on that equation), in practice the exchange rate with moneychangers could be 17 or 18 asses, depending on whether one was selling or buying denarii. This extra charge was the commission, part of which at least went to the city, and, although its rate varied, as we can see from inscriptions and papyri, it was fairly universal, even in normal times. In abnormal times the rate could, of course, fluctuate even more wildly. During the desperate siege of Jerusalem in AD 69/70 prices shot up; everything sold for gold and aurei became relatively so plentiful that "you could buy for 12 denarii coins formerly worth 25" (Josephus, *Wars* 5.550). This was exceptional, but generally the nature of the system of exchange and the obvious abuses to which it was susceptible enables us to understand why being a moneychanger was a jealously guarded monopoly and why it was thought to be of such importance to the economic stability of the empire that the coinage should circulate smoothly. In AD 210, the emperor Septimius Severus passed regulations for the city of Mylasa in Asia, laying down tough penalties for those who illegally exchanged or bought currency – for a slave, a whipping and six months in jail, and so on.

"For the safety of the city is endangered through the evil-doing and wickedness of a certain few, who trample on and rob the public interest, and through whose power a kind of exchange has established itself in our market, which keeps the city from possessing the necessaries of life, while many are in need and the state in want" (*OGIS* 515).

103

A crisis of confidence?

Thus the state tried to protect the coinage from many forms of abuse, and particularly from forgery and the malpractices of moneychangers, by specific provisions against particular abuses as they arose and by general legislation against forgery and other illegal activities. Savage penalties were generally in force against those who refused to accept coins with the imperial image (*vultu principum signatam monetam*) and against those who tampered with the coinage in any way, by "falsifying, washing, melting, clipping, breaking or injuring" it. These penalties included deportation, condemnation to the mines or even crucifixion (Paul, *Sententiae* 5.25.1). Normally such sanctions were not necessary: the saying of Epictetus quoted at the beginning of chapter four makes it clear that the indirect use of the design with its moral appeal to the power of the emperor and the threat of treason if it were abused was usually sufficient to maintain public confidence. Only with the steep debasement of the coinage in the third century did serious problems of confidence arise, particularly in Egypt, where many papyri reflect a new distinction, apparently between new and old coins. Another papyrus perhaps shows that there was a general crisis of confidence:

"From Aurelius Ptolemaeus also called Nemesianus, strategus of the Oxyrhynchite nome [Egypt]. Since the public officials have assembled and accused the bankers of the banks of exchange of having closed them on account of their unwillingness to accept the divine coins of the Emperors (*to theion ton Sebaston nomisma*), it has become necessary that an injunction should be issued to all the owners of the banks to open them, and to accept and exchange all coin except the absolutely spurious and counterfeit, and not only to them, but to all who engage in business transactions of any kind whatever, knowing that if they disobey this injunction they will experience the penalties ordained for them previously by his highness the Prefect [of Egypt]" (*POxy* 1411, AD 260).

PART THREE

Chapter Six

Inflation

Introduction

Was inflation a feature of the Roman world? If so, how important
was it? What can usefully be said about it? One should at the
outset stress the word "usefully"; for one can only explore a
question like this to a limited degree, as there is very little data.
Although the Romans made some attempt to set state budgets
and keep economic statistics in a limited way, none of this
information has survived. Consequently one can hardly do any
more than draw in a general, rather sketchy, outline of what was
actually happening.

First of all, what is meant by inflation? Inflation has many
different technical meanings to an economist, but here I shall use
the word in the most common sense of a rise in prices. What
actually does cause a steady increase in prices? Fisher's equation
states simply that $mv = pq$; that is m (money) times v (its velocity
of circulation) equals p (price) times q (the quantity of goods in
circulation). Most of the elements of this equation are clear,
except perhaps for v. The essential point is that if one group of
people use a finite amount of coin more frequently than another
group of people, who might for instance hoard it away
somewhere, then the amount of money in use in the first group is
in fact much greater than in the second group, even though both
groups have the same actual quantity of coins. Otherwise the
equation is fairly straightforward. For instance, if money
increases, for example by a government decision to print and
issue more notes or, in the ancient world, to make more coins,
then prices will rise in proportion to the increase in money,
providing everything else remains the same. Again, if more
goods come on to the market, for example if there happens to be
a very good harvest, then the price will fall, if the other factors in
the equation remain the same.

Can Fisher's equation be applied to the ancient Roman world?
Of course there are immediately all sorts of problems, mostly
stemming from the lack of information already mentioned about

105

Inflation

the quantity of goods in circulation within the Roman empire, and more importantly, whether it varied significantly from period to period. Little is known about alterations in the velocity of the exchange of money. Thus I shall assume rashly, but in common with most discussions of the subject, that v(elocity) and q(uantity of goods) remained broadly constant, and concentrate on the remaining elements, m(oney) and p(rices).

There is some evidence of prices in the Roman world, mostly drawn from inscriptions and particularly papyri, although this evidence is very scattered and uneven in nature and quality. Two main problems arise. Firstly, the prices for some commodities are so rare that there simply is no other price recorded on another occasion to allow comparison. Secondly, there is the question of quality and its effect on prices; a donkey whose price is recorded in AD 100 might have been old and worked out, whereas the one for which a price is recorded in AD 200 might be young and fit. This problem of quality also affects wheat and wine: the two commodities whose prices are most useful, since bread and wine were the basic foodstuffs of the ancient world and so their price tends to be recorded more frequently. But the price of wheat is notoriously liable to seasonal variation, for example, if there has been a good or a bad harvest, while the price of wine must have varied enormously with its quality, as it does today. The effect of all this is to make price comparisons full of problems and uncertainties.

As for m, we also have some idea about the amount of money in circulation, thanks to the die studies described in chapter five. On the basis of these we can calculate roughly how many coins were minted and in circulation. Using this information and ignoring v and q effectively reduces Fisher's equation to what is generally known as the quantity theory of money. According to this theory there is a simple and direct relation between the amount of money and prices. The greater the amount of money, the higher the prices, and vice versa: compare the situation in this country during the 1970s, when the sharp inflation was generally blamed on the government's continuing printing of more pound notes.

This quantity theory is perhaps rather obvious, and so it is no surprise that the Romans too were aware of it. There are two famous instances. After the defeat of Antony and Cleopatra at the battle of Actium in 31 BC, the emperor Augustus captured so much plunder that when it was brought back to Italy for his triumph in 29 the injection of so much wealth into the economy caused a large increase in the price of land. As Suetonius wrote in

his life of Augustus, "when he brought the treasuries of the
Egyptian kings to Rome at his Alexandrian triumph, so much
cash (*tanta copia nummariae rei*) passed into public hands that
the interest rate on loans dropped sharply, while property values
soared" (*Augustus* 41). Less than twenty years earlier, in the 40s
BC, exactly the opposite had taken place. At the height of the civil
war between the supporters of Julius Caesar and those of
Pompey there was a shortage of coin, a "nummorum caritas" as
Cicero called it in one of his letters. Cicero also commented on a
consequence, a fall in the price of land: less money, lower prices.

As well as indicating a knowledge of the quantity theory of
money in the short term, these anecdotes illustrate two points
about the nature of money in the ancient world and the
government's ability to control it. Money was much narrower in
extent in the Roman world than today, when the wide range of
sophisticated financial systems enables the stock of money to
consist of much more than the banknotes and coins which
physically exist. This is supplemented by the huge amount of
credit given by organisations like banks and building societies, a
credit which vastly increases the quantity of money available and
bears no relation to the amount of actual cash, although
governments may well from time to time try to restrict it. The
financial institutions of the ancient world were much less
sophisticated, however, and borrowing and lending were on a
comparatively small scale. This effectively reduced the amount of
money available to the equivalent of cash, rather than cash plus
bank lending as today, and, as the Romans had no banknotes, this
meant the quantity of coins actually in existence. Secondly,
although the Romans were obviously – at least in practice – aware
of the quantity theory, there seems to have been little ability on
their part to control its effects. In the 40s BC, for instance, Caesar
passed a law forbidding anyone to hoard more than 15,000
denarii, in an attempt to drive coins out of hoards and back into
circulation. This law, I would have thought, was likely to be as
ineffective as it was unenforceable. More successful perhaps was
the restoration of liquidity, which resulted from the regular issue
of large quantities of high value gold coins from 46 BC (previously
only silver had been minted). On other occasions one hears of
attempts to restrict the flow of precious metal from Italy (in 63
BC), or a ban on exporting coin from one province to another
where it would be worth more (in the fourth century); not
infrequently one hears of extra cash provided by the emperor to
help those unable to pay their debts due to a shortage of coin (*see*
chapter five). Yet in all this the overall impression is that these

were all short-term solutions to short-term crises, which occurred with an unpredictable regularity, and that there was no long-term strategy, or as we would call it, monetary policy, behind it.

But when we turn to the direct examination of inflation and the evidence for it at Rome we should not consider so much short-term crises of the type just mentioned, but long-term movements of price. For reasons which will become obvious, the discussion of inflation falls naturally into the two parts of the denarius coinage and of the later empire; firstly, the period down to about the middle of the third century, and secondly the following century and a half up to about AD 400.

The denarius period

During the first period there was a gradual and fairly steady increase in price levels. This can be seen in a number of ways. During the Republic, in the second century BC, a whole series of fines which had originally been expressed in asses were reassessed in the same number of sestertii. As a sestertius was then worth 2½ asses, this was an increase of 250%. At the same time, property qualifications, the amount of wealth one had to possess to qualify for membership of the class of Roman knights or senators, were reassessed in the same way, similarly suggesting the same increase in price levels. Now our knowledge of these early increases is very limited, and cannot really be enlarged as we have no records of prices; the few prices that do survive occur in later annalists and are not likely to be reliable since they concerned the far distant past which the annalists wished to portray as a golden age.

We can start to use the evidence of prices, and indeed of coins, from the later second century BC. The problems which may arise when comparing different prices mentioned on papyri or inscriptions have already been mentioned, but after making some allowances for these the following picture emerges, based mainly on the price of wheat. From the second century BC to the first century BC prices approximately doubled; then they seem to have remained more or less stable into the first century AD, but from then until the middle of the third century AD there was another steady if gradual increase: an increase of about 50% by the second century and by a further 100% by about AD 260. Thus if we were to set a notional price index for the Roman world at 100 in the second century BC, it stood at 200 in the age of Caesar a hundred years later, at 300 by the end of the second century AD, and at 600 in the time of Gallienus, in about AD 260. On the face of it this is a large increase; but we should remember that it took place over some 450 years: if the rise had been constant during that period, it would have averaged out at a simple annual rate of only about 1% per annum. Expressed as an average annual compound rate, however, it was virtually zero.

We can also trace this increase by looking at the smallest coin denominations generally in use at a given time, in much the same way that we can observe that the abandonment of low value coins like the half penny and the introduction of large ones like the pound coin are consequences of price inflation. Small denominations become increasingly useless as prices rise and have to be replaced by larger ones. This also happened in the Roman world. During the period in question the monetary system was based on the denarius, subdivided into four sestertii or sixteen asses; each of these asses was also subdivided into fractions of the as. In the second century BC the smallest common coin was the sextans or one-sixth of an as (**24**); by the first century its rôle had been filled by the quadrans or one-quarter of an as (**63**), which was for instance the price of admission to the public baths. In the second century AD this was in turn replaced by the semis (**96**) or one-half of an as (*see* chapter three). This change from a sixth to a half is the same, threefold, increase which was just noted in prices over the same period. During this period there was also a corresponding shift in the coin most commonly in daily use, from the as (**74, 87**) to the sestertius or four-as piece (**90, 95, 98**).

How are we to account for this increase? The answer seems simply to lie in an increase in the quantity of money, or actual coin, in circulation. This rose both because, and one might add in spite of, the development of Rome from a relatively small power dominating central Italy at the beginning of our period to become the ruler of the Mediterranean world, from Spain to the Syrian desert and from Britain to the south of Egypt. To achieve this position Rome was involved at first in almost continual warfare, which was for the most part successful. There were two main consequences of this. Firstly, the wars required huge numbers of soldiers and quantities of military equipment. All of these had to be paid for, thus bringing an increase in the amount of coin minted and in circulation, as can be seen from Fig. 6.1. Secondly, Rome's conquests brought much treasure, like Augustus's plunder after the defeat of Antony and Cleopatra at the battle of Actium, and this contributed to the amount of money in the economy, particularly as plunder was often sold off and the proceeds distributed to the populace.

Inflation

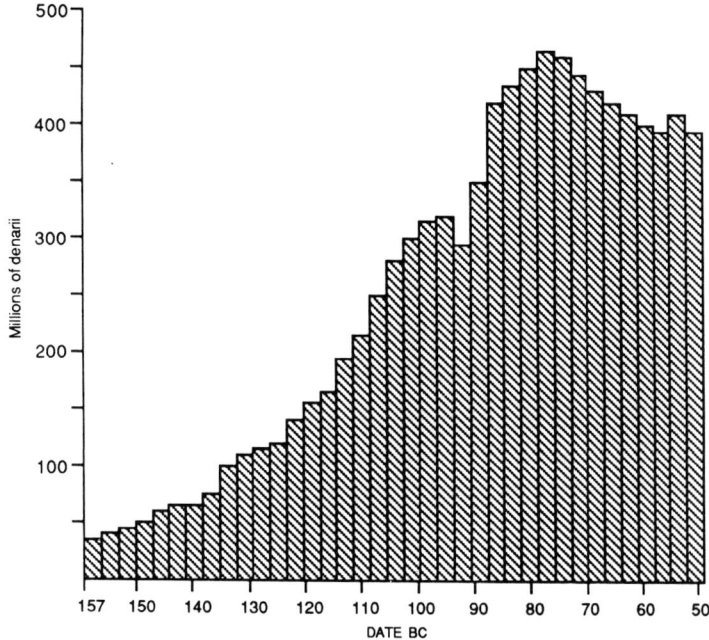

FIG. 6.1 *The Growth and Decline of the Roman Money Supply*
Roman silver coins in circulation between 157 and 50 BC, in millions of
denarii, by three-year periods. (From K. Hopkins, Journal of Roman
Studies *1980, 109, FIG. 2.)*

I should now explain the remark that the growth of money also took place despite Rome's expansion. As a result of her conquests the geographical size of the Roman world and economy was enormously increased; it may also be the case that there was also an increase in the intensity of economic activity, since it seems that there may have been an increase in the level of trade during the period. The effect of this increase in the rôle required of money should have been to limit the inflationary tendency, since although there was more money it was having to do more: in a loose sense the q or "quantity of goods" element in Fisher's equation was greatly increased in value, and mathematically this should have reduced the value of p, the price. Despite the offsetting tendency, however, prices did increase, as we have seen. The conclusion must be that there was more money around, so things cost more and people got paid more. For instance, in the second century BC a soldier was paid 110 or 125 denarii every year; a hundred years later his pay had doubled to

110

225; another hundred years later it had increased to 300 and by the third century it had increased again, probably to 600 denarii per annum. It is obviously no coincidence that these figures correspond exactly to the notional price rise index that I have just constructed.

The late empire

Such is the broad outline of the history of price inflation under the Roman Republic and early Roman empire down to the middle of the third century: a fairly steady but tiny increase. From this date, however, and for the next hundred and fifty years, the picture dramatically changed. The Romans experienced a period of what can be called hyper-inflation.

Let us look again at the prices recorded (mainly in papyri) for wheat. In the twenty-five years or so between about AD 270 and 290 the price of wheat increased by a factor of about five. During the same period, as far as we can tell, other prices increased by as much or even more. For instance, recorded prices for slaves and donkeys show increases over the same period of 800 to 1500%. I should stress that there are very few prices on which to base these statistics, and the figures must be seen as indicative rather than in any way exact.

In the fourth century even more staggering increases took place, although again any attempt at quantification should be regarded as crude in view of the nature of the evidence. That said, let us take as an example the price of gold. In 301 the maximum legally permitted price was 72,000 denarii a pound (it had been worth about 1000 in the early empire); by 313 the official price was 110,000 denarii, and in about 317 the market price was 430,000 denarii. We do not unfortunately have any exact figures immediately thereafter, but later in the century, perhaps in 388, a pound of gold was worth no less than 3,000,000,000 or, we would say today, 3 billion denarii. It is no wonder that accounts came to be kept in myriads or 10,000s of denarii rather than simple denarii as before. We cannot follow the course of this price increase in any detail, although it seems that there may have been a sharp rise in prices in the 350s, and that there may have been a period of some twenty years between 360 and 380 when prices rose a hundredfold. Taking the fourth century as a whole, we are talking of an increase in prices of about 30,000 times over 100 years or an average annual compound inflation rate of as much as 11%.

What brought about this sharp rise in the late third century, and the even greater increases in the fourth? Leaving on one side the view that there was a reduction in the quantity of goods in circulation, a view for which there is no proof, there seem to have been two main causes; firstly, a change in the nature of money, and, secondly, a change in the quantity of money in circulation.

Firstly, the nature of money in the Roman world. As described in chapter three, the basis of the coinage in the early empire had been the silver coin, the denarius, later joined, from about 46 BC, by the gold aureus. These coins stood in fixed relationship to each other, with the aureus being worth 25 denarii, and the same applied to the smaller denominations (for example there were 16 bronze asses to each denarius). These relationships were enforced by the government. As a result the value of the coinage was directly linked to the value of the precious metals gold and silver; so if there was a tendency for prices to rise and for the purchasing power of the coins to fall, this fall would be restrained by the intrinsic bullion value of the gold and silver coins. Their purchasing power would also tend to rise as the general increase in commodity prices also pushed up the price and value of gold and silver with other commodities. This oversimplification is not of course the whole story, since it seems that the face value of the coins was rather higher than their intrinsic value, and this would tend to weaken the link between the rise in the price of precious metals and the enhanced purchasing power of the coins.

In the third century, however, two things had taken place, which combined to remove this link altogether. Firstly the silver coinage had been progressively debased, by the addition of ever increasing amounts of copper to the silver from which the coins were made (*see* Fig. 6.2). Eventually, by about 270, the main silver coin contained little more than a trace of silver, only 1 or 2% at most. This debasement seems to have been brought about by a shortage of silver; it became necessary to put less and less silver into each coin if the stock of available silver was not sufficient to provide for an increase in the number of coins needed to pay the army or whatever. This was a tendency which had begun in the first century AD, but became exacerbated in the third century.

The shortage of precious metals also affected the gold coinage. Large quantities of gold coins had been minted in the first and second centuries, but the scale of minting was steadily reduced in the third century, as we can see not only from the rarity of the coins today, but also from the fact that third-century gold hoards are tiny, and that such gold coins are rarely found as chance finds in comparison with earlier coins. By the middle of the century the quantity minted and in circulation appears to have been so small that it can have played practically no part in the currency of the empire. Gold was so scarce that it too was even debased for several years from 253 (*see* Fig. 7.1), an event unpredecented in Roman monetary history.

The result of these changes to the gold and silver coinage was that the currency of the empire became almost completely a token coinage. The departure of precious metal left the coinage without any real or intrinsic value, and thus the link between the rising level of prices and the rising purchasing power of coinage metal was broken, leaving the currency at the mercy of the

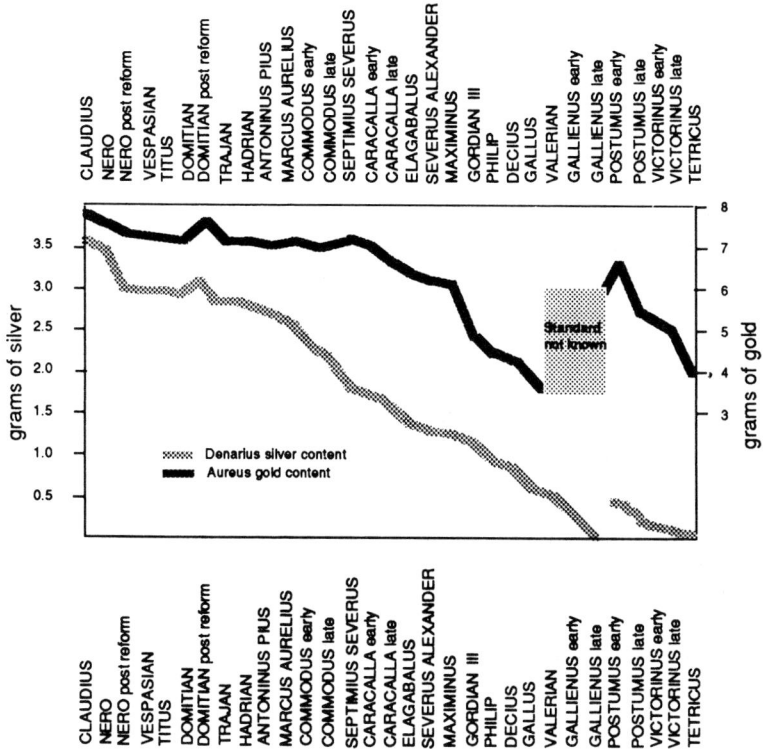

FIG. 6.2 *Gold and Silver Standards in the Empire*
The decline in the fineness of the silver and the weight of the aureus were more or less parallel until the late third century. (After J. Casey Coinage in Roman Britain *FIG. 2, but omitting gold standards for Valerian, Gallienus and Claudius as these are uncertain.)*

market. The purchasing power of the coins would not increase, so while they remained tariffed in denarii, the fact that prices rose in terms of denarii led to the need for more and more coins, and hence rampant inflation.

This state of affairs seems to have been recognised shortly after 250, when the government abandoned the attempt to keep the link between gold and silver coins, the previous history of which can be seen from the graph which shows that the weight of the gold coin had declined in step with the debasement of the silver (*see* Fig. 6.2). From 253, however, the gold was debased and the weights of gold coins fluctuated wildly, and apparently independently of the silver. This suggests that it was at this period that the equation of so many silver coins to the gold one was dropped. Some stability returned in about 270, when the purity of the gold coin was restored. This may perhaps be the date of the introduction of the solidus, a coin name first attested twenty years later in the 290s, whose meaning perhaps reflects the purity of the coin and refers to a coin worth its weight in gold, i.e. with a value of whatever that amount of gold was worth at any given time. The dropping of a formal link between the gold and the rest of the currency would of course exacerbate the token nature of the coinage, as it would remove such support as the value of the small-scale gold coinage had been able to give to the value of the currency at large, and thus the inflation of the time would be encouraged.

If this change in the nature of money can help explain the sudden rise of prices at the end of the third century, then we still have to provide some reason for the acceleration of price rises which is attested in the fourth century. The explanation is probably again to be seen in terms of the quantity theory; there was once more a rise in the amount of money in circulation. This happened mainly in two ways. Firstly, the state seems to have made no real attempt to limit the amount of base metal currency issued, which would have been the only way to hold its depreciation in check. In fact, quite the reverse seems the case: money was produced in large quantities for a variety of reasons, for making such state payments as were made in coin and particularly to enable the government to retrieve as much gold for itself as possible. This retrieval was effected both by the compulsory purchase of gold at prices fixed by the government itself and by the provision of large quanitities of bronze coin to the moneychangers, who brought gold coins for the government from the public at fixed rates of exchange, both in the capital and probably also in the provinces.

Combined with this increase in the quantity of base metal coinage was an increase in the quantity of gold, as gold coinage was revived during the fourth century and returned to the position it had enjoyed in the early empire. The remonetisation of gold seems to have been stepped up by Constantine the Great (306–37). As the author of a fourth-century pamphlet wrote, "in the time of Constantine extravagant public expenditure displaced copper (which was previously considered of great value) with gold in transactions of low value" (Anon., *de rebus bellicis* 2). This minting of gold was made possible by Constantine's seizure of his enemies' treasuries, and particularly of the huge treasures previously locked up in pagan temples, which he liberated on his conversion to Christianity. The process continued throughout the century, and gold became particularly plentiful in the middle of the century, just when price rises seem to have been at their steepest. We can see how common gold had again become in a variety of ways. Gold coins played an increasing role in imperial laws of the century, as more and more they were specified as the medium in which fines were to be paid. They are also mentioned more frequently in the everyday transactions recorded on the papyri in Egypt, and tend again to turn up as chance finds more commonly than in the third century. The effect of this remonetisation of gold cannot be overestimated in calculating the total amount of money in circulation, given the huge relative value of gold. In the 350s, for instance, the minting of a single gold coin would have increased the amount of money in circulation by its current value of about 1.5 million denarii. Moreover, from about that time until about AD 400, there was also a substantial coinage of silver (**161**), additionally contributing to the quantity of money.

Remedies and consequences

Thus the increase in prices in the late empire may be accounted for by looking at what was happening to money at the time. But what were the consequences of this high price inflation? What did the government do about it, if anything? Did it affect everyday life? If so, how did people cope? These questions are surprisingly difficult to answer, as there is not much evidence to go on, and it is open to rather divergent interpretations.

Firstly, let us look at the government's attitude. It is, I think, clear that the emperors were concerned by the price inflation and attempted to meet it in various ways. One way was to revalue their coins upwards so that every coin would have a greater face value; as if, for instance, it was decreed that every 10p coin should be worth 20p. We are lucky enough through the accidents of survival to know that this definitely happened on at least one occasion, since an inscription was found a few years ago at Aphrodisias in south-west Turkey, and we may suspect that the same thing also happened on other occasions. The inscription (*see* Plate 17) records a decision taken in 301 by the emperor Diocletian, and refers specifically to the doubled face value, the "geminata potentia', of coins. Unfortunately the inscription does not record Diocletian's reason for doing this, but it seems obvious enough: in a period of rapidly rising prices it was an attempt to increase the usefuless of the coins in existence. Cynics may observe that it was also intended at a stroke to double the value of the government's holdings in cash. Exactly the reverse tactic was tried by the emperor Licinius about twenty years later, when it seems possible that he halved the face value of the coinage; if so, it was presumably reduced from 25 denarii to the 12½ which appears on some of his coins (**144**). This may well be the occasion referred to by a letter preserved in a papyrus, which was written by someone in the know called Dionysius to one of his officials called Apion: "The divine fortune of our lords has ordained that the Italian coinage be reduced to half a nummus. Be quick therefore to spend all the Italian coinage you have and buy for me goods of every description at whatever price you find them" (*PRyl* 607).

Licinius's intentions were obviously more sophisticated than Diocletian's. He presumably hoped that by reducing the face value of the coinage, he would cut the amount of money in half; hence according to the quantity theory, prices should fall. Unfortunately we do not know how successful his attempt was, if at all. There is some evidence for a fall in the price of gold in the East in 324 (*POxy* 1430), but the details of his reform are not clear.

There were other official acts which should have restricted the amount of money, when certain classes of coin were demonetised, that is to say, declared worthless. Consequently, people had to get rid of these coins or find that they were worth nothing, and we can see from coin hoards that on a number of occasions, for instance in about 300 and about 354, huge quantities of coin were removed from circulation. Now it is not at all clear, however, that the motive for these withdrawals was anti-inflationary, since in each case they were accompanied by the issue of new coins with presumably even greater face values. We might suspect that these withdrawals took place in the attempt to instill confidence in the new coins by removing the old with their lower value, just as the old penny was removed from circulation when it was replaced by the new penny which was less impressive, but worth twice as much. One gets the impression that this tactic, of occasional reforms comprising the issue of new higher valued coins, was the government's normal response to the price inflation of the fourth century. The typical pattern that seems to emerge is that such a reform would be made; prices would continue to rise; the government would reduce the weight of the coin to enable it to make more from the same quantity of bullion, as more were required due to the increase in prices; this increase in the amount of coin in circulation would fuel the price inflation, and eventually prompt another reform in turn when the face value of the reduced coins became negligible. This was a way of coping with the effects of inflation, and was not of course an attempt to stop it. Compare modern Israel, with its rampant inflation creating and destroying five coinage systems in thirty-eight years. The only attempts to stop inflation in the fourth century were the one by Licinius, already mentioned, and another by Diocletian in 301 which must go down as one of history's most colossal failures. Diocletian's attempt to end inflation consisted of trying to make it illegal, by establishing a maximum legal price for virtually all commodities. Huge inscriptions were set up all over the empire (today they survive from ten different locations, mostly in Greece, Asia Minor and Egypt), to stipulate the maximum prices allowed for an immense number of different commodities, from gold bullion to peas and beans, and the maximum wages allowed for a large variety of occupations, from farm workers to professors. The seriousness with which Diocletian viewed the problem can be seen from the fact that the death penalty was stipulated for anyone who breached the provisions of the edict. Death was also laid down for anyone who simply withdrew goods from the market to avoid the provisions of the edict, an obvious move if one could not get a good price. However, a contemporary commentator (Lactantius, *de mort. pers.* 7.6) tells us that this is exactly what happened; there was a widespread withdrawal of goods from the market, leading to even higher price levels and the subsequent abandonment of the edict.

Although the benefit of hindsight shows us the futility of the huge investment of time and effort which went into Diocletian's price edict, we are lucky that it survives to give us such revealing information about an emperor's attitude to price inflation. The list of prices is preceded by a long introduction, which together with the use of the death penalty illustrates the seriousness with which Diocletian took the matter. He says, for instance, "Who is so hard and devoid of human feeling that he cannot perceive that in the commerce carried on in the markets or involved in the daily life of cities immoderate prices are so widespread that the unbridled passion for gain is lessened by neither supplies nor fruitful years?" Or, again, "Everyone knows that . . . not just in every village or town, but on every road, . . . the profiteer extorts prices for goods, not merely fourfold or eightfold, but such that human speech is incapable of describing the price or the act; and sometimes a single purchase by a soldier deprives him of his bonus and salary, so that the contributions of the whole world towards our armies fall to the abominable profits of thieves."

If then the government seems to have been unable or uninterested in controlling inflation, how did it manage its own finances? In a situation where the currency was rapidly depreciating in value, it was clearly not in the government's interests to accept payment in it, since the value would have fallen substantially by the time it was spent. There were two ways around this problem. First of all the government insisted that a number of transactions were performed in gold, by assessing the payment of at least some taxes, for example on trades, in gold. The government would in this way be able to preserve the value of its finances. This is presumably why it developed various methods for ensuring a steady flow of gold into its own coffers; we have already commented on the system by which it minted bronze to buy back gold through the moneychangers at fixed rates. These rates obviously went out of date very rapidly, and on occasion had to be revised upwards to the market price, as otherwise no one was prepared to sell their gold coins (Symmachus, *Rel.* 29 of 384). The government also collected gold in other ways, for instance the compulsory purchase of gold bullion from landowners who were required to provide gold on some regular basis for resale to the government at fixed rates. Since the value of gold was free like that of other commodities to rise in price, it was clearly in the government's interest to make as much use of gold in its finances as possible.

A second way in which the government could maintain its own financial position was to levy taxes and make payments in kind, rather than in cash. This seems mainly to have taken the form of the local provision of things like corn, wine, meat and clothes to army units, replacing at least in part the payment of coin in direct taxes. This arrangement, known as the "annona", involved the collection of taxes in kind, and also the payment of government expenses in kind, for inasmuch as they were made directly to the army, they also replaced state payments in cash.

It is no doubt possible to exaggerate the extent to which the government reverted to this economy of kind and gold instead of the economy of coined copper money, and undoubtedly some taxes, for example on transport, and some payments continued to be made in base metal coinage. Yet it is clear that in the two ways outlined above the government tried to minimise the effect of inflation on itself. But in what ways did the ordinary man in the street feel its effects?

We know that rents were sometimes paid in kind and that some private workers also received payment in kind, as, for instance, was the case with some agricultural workers in Egypt in 338, but this seems to be unusual and it seems that most transactions continued to be made in cash, and as such were subject to inflation. In the reign of Aurelian, for instance, we hear in a papyrus of the high price for woven goods, "because of the increased price of raw materials and the increased wages of workmen" (*POxy* 1414) – a consideration familiar enough to all of us. A second example concerns official salaries and pay. Although soldiers received their living in kind through the annona, papyri such as *PBeattyPanop* 2 show that they continued to receive cash payment for the stipendium, which appears in AD 300 to have been the same 600 denarii it had been a hundred years earlier. A fairly derisory sum perhaps, in an age when an egg cost a denarius or the average daily manual wage was perhaps around twenty denarii, yet its fall in purchasing power was the main reason for Diocletian's attempt to curb prices with his edict, as we saw in the passage quoted above. Civil servants too received cash payments; a certain Theophanes in the 320s and 330s (*PRyl* 617–51) was paid in bronze coin and conducted business in it. Thus anyone who was dependent on a cash income was vulnerable to the effects of inflation, the more so the greater the proportion of his income that was paid in cash.

Some people stood to gain from inflation. Then, as now, anyone in debt benefited from the rapid depreciation of the capital sum he borrowed; compare the effect on people with mortgages of the increase in house prices in the late 1970s. Lenders of course tried in turn to preserve their position by building in anti-inflation devices into their agreements. An example would be that if, say, a sum of money was loaned on the security of a certain commodity, then the repayment required would be linked in some way to the value of that commodity at the time of repayment.

Our knowledge of such devices is of course limited to individual incidents, and a far more important question is the more general effect that inflation may have had on the social structure of the late Roman world. There are many different views on this today. One view holds that it caused enormous changes. The opposite holds that the effect should have been minimal, since although it is true that prices did rise in terms of denarii, they did not rise in real terms, in terms of gold or other commodities. One can demonstrate, for instance, that wages and prices, converted from the currency of the day into gold, did not really differ from the second century to the fourth; Hence it can be argued that the effect of inflation is more apparent than real. Yet it has already been suggested that the more one had to deal in base metal currency the more one suffered from inflation; it is therefore crucial to ask to what extent people were forced so to deal. It is not possible to be precise here, but two considerations may be helpful. One is the case of a centurion who died in the early fourth century; the money he left in gold and bronze currency is recorded (*POxy* 3307) and one can calculate that about 80% of his money was in bronze and only 20% in gold, yet surely he would have tried to maximise his holdings in gold. This suggests that gold was not freely available. A more general point is suggested by the consideration that more than 70% of landowners seem to have owned less land than was necessary to produce enough yield to be worth a gold coin. The implication seems to be clear, that at least 70% of the rural population were excluded from the currency of gold coin, and so were at the mercy of bronze coinage and its inflation.

On this basis one could draw a picture of landowners who were gradually dispossessed of their land so that they could raise gold to pay their taxes, a process which would have been exacerbated if, as has been suggested, the level of taxation in the fourth century was higher than earlier. Against this point of view, however, one can argue that the evidence for heavier taxes is not clear cut, and that, so far as we can tell, there seems to have been no general abandonment of the land. Indeed it is possible to think of the fourth century as a period of prosperity; there is some support for this from archaeological evidence and literary sources. These indications might find some confirmation in the consideration that commodity values do not seem to have increased in terms of gold, despite the large increase in gold coinage and its availability. According to Fisher's equation, this would only make sense if the increase in gold was offset by a similar increase in the quantity of goods, indicating increased levels of economic growth and prosperity.

PLATE 17

Inscription found at Aphrodisias, Turkey, containing part of
the letter from Diocletian revaluing the coinage in 301.

PLATE 18

132

133

134

135

136

137

138

139

PLATE 19

140

141(X2)

142

143

144

145

146

147

148

149

150

PLATE 20

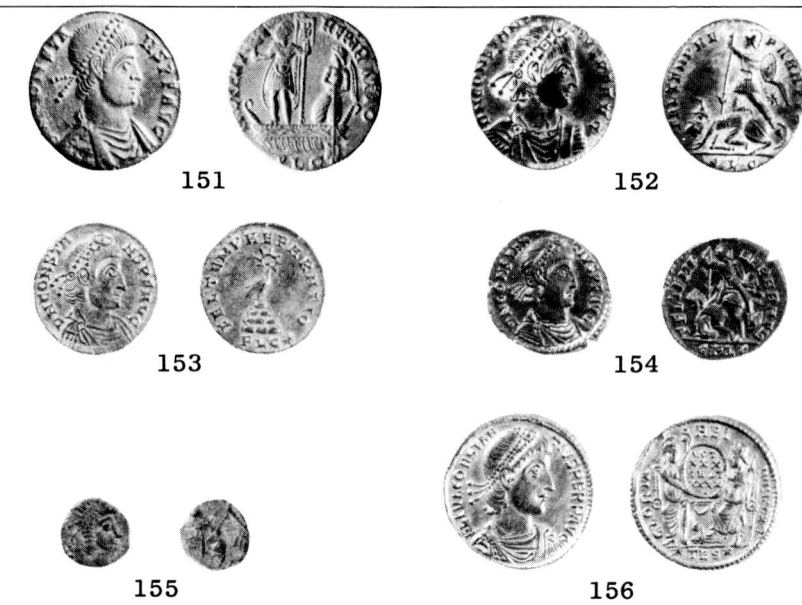

151 152

153 154

155 156

The Water Newton, Cambs. (1974), Treasure Trove.
Department of Prehistoric and Romano-British
Antiquities, British Museum

PLATE 21

The insignia of the Comes Sacrarum Largitionum.
Bodleian Library, Oxford.

PLATE 22

157

158

159

160(X½)

161

162

163

164

PLATE 23

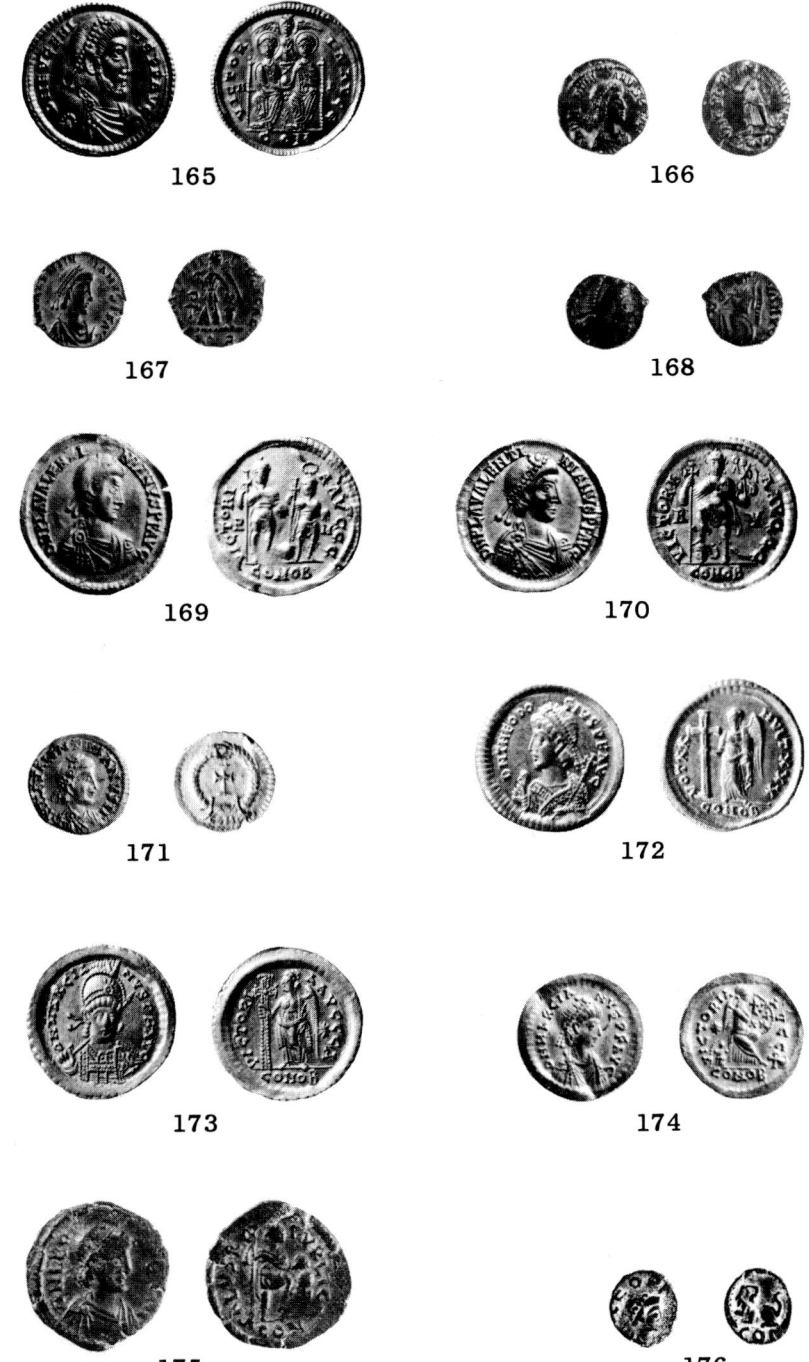

165

166

167

168

169

170

171

172

173

174

175

176

PLATE 24

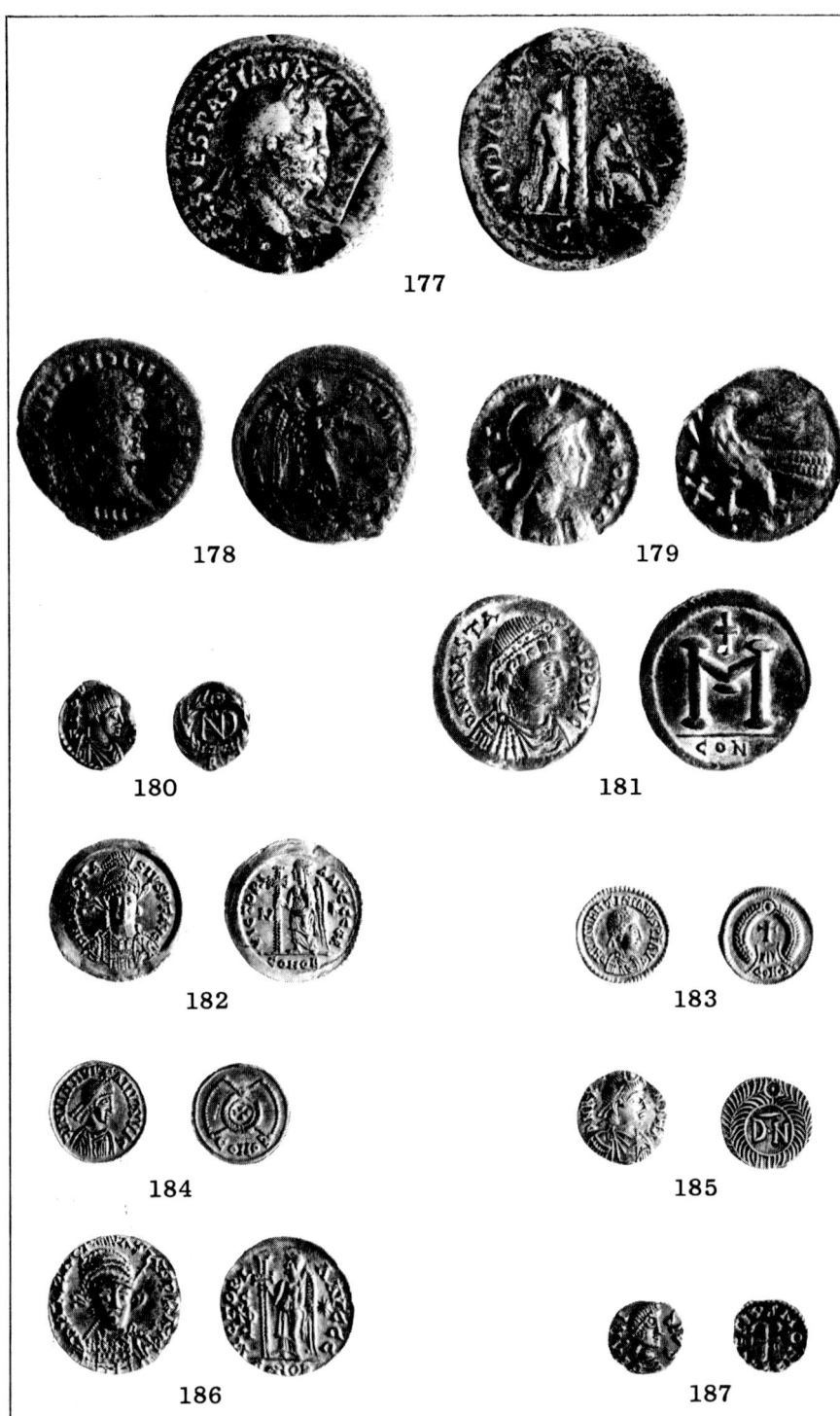

177

178   179

180   181

182   183

184   185

186   187

Inflation

These are perhaps the more extreme of the spectrum of possible views, and intermediate positions are also possible. One could think, for instance, that the shift from the pattern of a large number of small landowners in late Roman Egypt to a pattern of much fewer and larger landowners in Byzantine Egypt could at least partially be explained by late Roman monetary history, along the lines indicated above, and that at the same time commercial wealth was more noticeably concentrated in fewer hands, giving rise to a picture of prosperity. At any rate, whatever the exact consequences of inflation, it seems likely that it did have some of the effects just described, and that it was not just a question of juggling with numbers and retariffing coins.

Chapter Seven

Monetary history

Fragmentation and crisis

In chapter six the two related and fundamental differences between the early and late Roman coinage were characterised, namely the abandonment of a fixed relationship between the gold and the silver which by now had become almost completely debased, and the minting of a gold coinage worth its bullion value. These differences were the result of the crisis in the coinage of the middle of the third century, brought on by rising prices and the minting of increased numbers of more and more base silver coin. Consequently the lower value bronze coinage had ceased throughout the empire by the 260s, while the capacity of the empire to produce the 'silver' radiate had been greatly expanded; the number of sections at the mint of Rome was doubled from six to twelve, sometimes marked on the coins, for example that of Gallienus marked with XII (**120**), and new mints were set up around the empire, for example in Siscia (**119**). As described in chapter three, the period that saw the greatest increase in the number of mints was the reign of Valerian (253–60) and that of Gallienus (260–68), although the network of mints continued to develop gradually over the next fifty years. Generally these new mints tended to be situated towards the frontiers, no doubt to facilitate the delivery of new coin to its main recipients, the armies situated there. Mints somewhere in Gaul (possibly Trier), at Milan, at Viminacium (temporarily) and at Antioch were established under Valerian; Siscia and Cyzicus were founded during the reign of Gallienus. Thus by the end of the 260s a fairly widespread mint system had been established, though not according to any systematic plan. The new mints had usually been set up in response to specific needs, such as Gallienus's campaigns in Gaul; nevertheless they tended, once founded, to become permanent.

The mint in Gaul, which is traditionally thought to have been at Cologne, although Trier is a more likely candidate, was taken over in 259 by the rebel Postumus (**121**), who founded a separate

Romano-Gallic empire, independent of Rome and comprising France, Britain, Germany and, initially, Spain. Postumus died in about 269, but he had four short-lived successors, Laelian, Marius, Victorinus and Tetricus (**122**), until the end of the breakaway empire in 274. The coinage of these emperors was originally produced at the single mint taken over from Gallienus, but a second mint was opened late in Postumus's reign, and the usurpers continued to use two mints until the end of their rule. Their mints produced the vast quantities of radiates that have survived in such huge numbers today: hoards of several thousand coins are normal, and several hoards of as many as thirty to fifty thousand have been recorded. The majority of these coins were produced by Victorinus and Tetricus; one can make a rough guess at their total output, using the method outlined in chapter five and on the basis of the die study that has been made for the short reign of Laelian. Using his coins as a sample, one can extrapolate the possible total output of Tetricus: a staggering several billion coins, in no more than about three years – a daily output of well over a million.

The integrity of the empire was not only under strain in the west during this period, but also elsewhere. In the Balkans, the usurpers Ingenuus (no coins), and then Regalian and his wife Dryantilla, briefly held power, but generally this area remained intact, and the main trouble came from further east. Uranius Antoninus seized power in Syria in 253–4, as did Macrian and Quietus in 260. More seriously, from the fall of Quietus in about 261 until 272, the whole of Syria and Egypt were under the control of the Palmyrene kings, at first Odenathus, and then after his death his queen Zenobia and her son Vabalathus. For most of this period, they recognised the suzerainty of Gallienus and his successors Claudius II and Aurelian, and the coins made at the mints of Antioch and Alexandria were solely in their names. At the end of their rule, however, a break occurred with the emperor Aurelian, which is reflected on the coinage of Antioch and Alexandria. At first coins in the names of both Aurelian and Vabalathus together were produced, but these were then followed by issues in the names of Vabalathus and Zenobia alone. It has been suggested that after the fall of Vabalathus and Zenobia, fear of retribution for these coins prompted a revolt of the moneyers at the mint of Antioch, which has been recorded by Malalas. The story of this revolt is not, however, clear, as other sources place it at Rome, where, it has been suggested, it was prompted by a similar cause, in this case fear of retribution for the minting of large numbers of coins in the name of the dead emperor Claudius II (such as **123**) rather than in that of the reigning Aurelian.

Aurelian's reforms

The reign of Aurelian (270–75) brought a substantial improvement to the fortunes of the empire. Aurelian managed to reunite the empire, by re-establishing his power over both the Romano-Gallic empire and the Palmyrene kings. He also, as described in chapter six, made far-reaching reforms to the coinage. It was in his reign that the fineness of the gold coinage (**125**) was restored to the high standards of purity it had enjoyed before the reigns of Valerian and Gallienus (Fig. 7.1), and it may well be the case that he established the system by which the gold coin was worth its bullion value. Aurelian was also the author of a reform which was to bring a twenty-year period of stability to the base silver coinage (even if not to the economy or to prices). Moreover, in place of the continually more debased and pathetic looking coinage (an important factor where confidence is concerned) he introduced a new, better manufactured, radiate with a broader flan size, a stable weight standard and and a fixed 5% content of silver, expressed on the coins as xxi (**126**) or, in Greek numerals, ka: twenty parts of bronze to one of silver. He also reorganised the network of mints (Fig. 7.2), reducing those in Gaul to one at Lyon, and moving the mint of Milan to Ticinum (Pavia). The mint at Siscia, however, continued, joined for a few years by one at Serdica and, very briefly, by another at an unknown Balkan location. Further east the mints of Cyzicus and Antioch continued to operate, and a new one was established in Syria, perhaps at Tripolis.

Yet it would be incorrect to think that Aurelian's reform transformed the monetary system of the empire. His new coins did not circulate uniformly throughout the empire. In some areas his new coins, conveniently known today as "aureliani", appear to have comprised the bulk of coinage in circulation. Elsewhere, however, they hardly appear to have circulated at all, and in their absence the currency comprised the radiates of Gallienus (**120**), Claudius II (**123**) and of the Romano-Gallic emperors (**122**), together with a mass of imitations (**124** is an imitation of **123**). The main area for the continuing circulation of radiates was northern Europe, but somewhat surprisingly they also spread in large quantities to north Africa and even to parts of Asia Minor. Wherever the new aureliani did not circulate, the radiates continued in circulation; thus, for example, coins of the

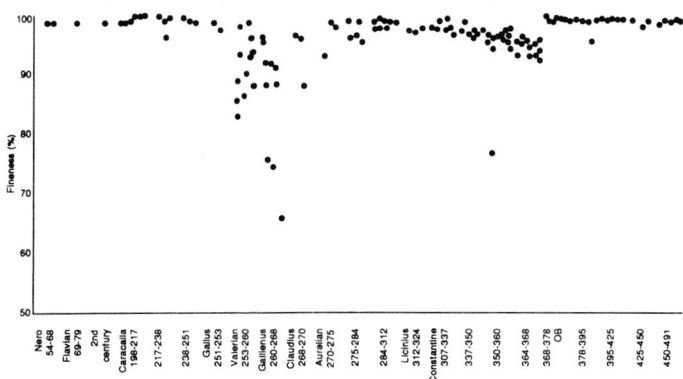

FIG. 7.1 *The Fineness of Roman Gold*
(*Data from* Cahiers Babelon 2, 1985, 82–6.)

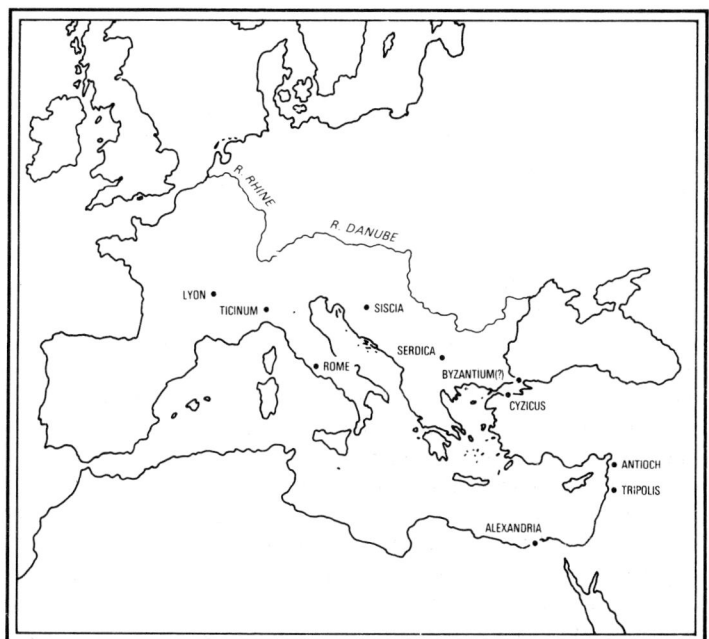

FIG. 7.2 *Mints under Aurelian*

Romano-Gallic emperors and imitations of them turn up regularly at north African sites like Sabrata or Asian ones like Aphrodisias, having travelled there from their origins in Gaul. It would be wrong, however, to suggest that the empire can be easily divided up in broad geographical areas, each representing the two sorts of circulation, since even within areas where one type of coin predominated, substantial finds of the other can be made: in Britain, for instance, there is a large hoard of 15,000 aureliani from Gloucester, while there is a hoard of barbarous radiates in the museum at Nicotera in Italy.

This difference in the circulation patterns of the two sorts of coin is very difficult to explain. We might suppose, for instance, that the supply of aureliani was not, for whatever reason, very good or adequate, and that the radiates travelled to fill the vacuum in circulation. This would explain their regular association with their imitations, which, as we have already seen, appear to have been produced when there was a shortage of coin. Another relevant factor may be the different denomination of radiates and aureliani. If for the sake of argument an aurelianus was valued at several radiates, then the tendency of the two sorts of coin not to mix in circulation might have been strengthened by their different face value.

From Diocletian's reforms to AD 318

Thus the coinage of the various parts of the Roman world from about 270 to about 285 was characterised by a relatively small production of gold, and the two patterns of circulation of debased silver. The subsequent reign of Diocletian (284–305) saw a number of reforms and changes to the monetary system of the empire, although we should not exaggerate his role as an innovator; essentially his achievement was to put the changes of the past decades on a more systematic basis. Diocletian's reforms were not all introduced together, but took place gradually over a period of some ten years. His first changes affected the gold coinage, and from early in the reign he stabilised the weight of the gold coin. In previous reigns, gold coins had been produced on a bewildering variety of different weights; in a sense, of course, this did not really matter, as the coins circulated at their bullion value and it was only necessary to weigh them to ascertain their value. But Diocletian had them made to a standard weight, some at about 4.6 grams or $\frac{1}{70}$ of a Roman pound (the coins were sometimes marked with an O, the Greek numeral for 70), but mostly at the standard of 5.3 grams or 1/60 of a pound (sometimes expressed with the relevant Greek numeral *Xi*: **134**, on a coin of his co-emperor Maximian). This weight standard was closely maintained until the time of Constantine the Great (307–337), who, no doubt for pressing financial reasons, reduced the standard to 1/72 (4.5 grams), which thereafter remained the standard weight of the gold coin until the end of the empire. Constantine introduced this new weight in the west, and spread it eastwards with his conquests of the rest of the empire, until with his final defeat of his last rival Licinius in 324 it became the universal gold coin of the Roman world. It has already been observed that the modern use of the word "solidus" to refer only to this coin of Constantine is mistaken (and misleading). It is certainly the name of Diocletian's gold coin, first attested in 296, and may well go back some years earlier (*see* chapter six).

Secondly, Diocletian restored a pure silver coinage to the empire, and silver coins were struck from the early 290s at a number of mints through the empire (**135**, from Rome). Unlike the gold, whose face value was its bullion value, the silver seems to have been considerably overvalued. The inscription about the coinage reform of 301 (*JRS* 1971.171) appears to give a value of 100 denarii to the silver coin (. . a]rgenteus centum denariis[. .), yet the contemporary price edict gives a maximum value of 6,000 denarii for a pound of silver. As the silver was struck at 96 coins to the pound (some of them use the numerals XCVI as their reverse design), the maximum theoretical value of the bullion it contained was 62.5 denarii; or, in fact, rather less, as the coins were not actually produced at their full weight. The new coins were produced in reasonably large numbers, to judge from their survival today, but they were not a successful coinage. Minting soon stopped, and thereafter the production of a common silver coinage lapsed for several decades. Secondly, the coins do not seem to have been much used, as when they occur in later hoards like those from Southsea or Kaiseraugst their unworn condition suggests that they had not circulated very much. Exactly why this silver coinage should have failed is not clear. Perhaps it was because they, unlike the gold coins, were tariffed at a fixed number of denarii. The increasing price of silver could soon have rapidly overtaken the face value of the coins and driven them out of circulation.

In his reforms both of the precious metal and the base metal coinages, Diocletian gave the empire its first uniform coinage, in terms of denominations, of the same designs, particularly the

"Spirit of the Roman People", the GENIO POPVLI ROMANI, on the base metal coinage (**136**), and of the similar pattern of circulation: in all these respects the coinage and currency of the empire was completely integrated. In the case of the base metal currency, this was achieved by two specific measures. First of all, the unusual status of Egypt with its closed currency system and its own particular coins (**130**, an Alexandrian "tetradrachm" of Diocletian) was brought to an end. Thereafter Egypt used the same sort of coins as the rest of the empire, and other coins were free to enter or leave it. Secondly, the division of the empire into the two distinct areas of base metal currency was ended, since the radiates and aureliani did not remain in circulation for more than a few years after a new base metal coinage was successfully inaugurated throughout the whole empire by Diocletian between 294 and 296.

These new base metal coins were not so much of an innovation as a variation on the coins introduced by Aurelian. In place of the aurelianus a new heavier coin of about 10 grams was introduced (**136**). Effectively this was just a higher denomination of the aurelianus, as it was theoretically composed of the same metal (5% silver: the same mark of fineness XXI occurs on some rare pieces). The coins are today generally but incorrectly known as *folles*. A *follis* was in fact a bag of coins of a certain value, rather than the name of a coin itself, and the term *nummus* is preferable. In addition to the nummus, smaller denominations were also produced in Italy and the east. There was a fractional piece with a radiate crown on the obverse, very much resembling the aurelianus and presumably in some way intended to replace it, although these "post-reform radiates" lacked the numerals XXI, which acknowledged that they now contained no silver. Finally, there was also a smaller piece with a laureate head, minted in only tiny quantities.

Much ink has been spilled over the question of the face value of these pieces, and elaborate calculations can be based on the quantity of the silver they contained and the price of that bullion as known from Diocletian's price edict. Yet the bullion price is not known for the actual period of the introduction of the coins; it would anyway be only a minimum, as the government was free to set the value of the coin anywhere above this minimum that it wished. That said, however, the face value of the new nummus was probably in the general region of 10 to 25 denarii, although greater precision does not seem possible at the moment.

Such is the main outline of the new coins produced by Diocletian, which basically systematised the reforms of Aurelian and set the pattern for the monetary history of the fourth century. We should, however, bear in mind that these coins represented a major part but not all of the money in use in the period. The gold (and later the silver) coins were supplemented by larger pieces, the so-called "medallions" (137, 141 and 157), which were really multiples of the gold coin, minted for presentation to senior military officers or important civil servants, as we can see from the three large hoards of gold deposited between about 270 and 315 in Corsica, Sicily and Arras. In each case the pattern of the pieces in the hoards shows that their owners had been the recipients of donatives or gifts from the emperor: for instance from Claudius II at Milan (Corsica), Maxentius at Rome (Sicily), or Constantius I at Trier, to celebrate his reconquest of Britain from the rebels Carausius and Allectus in 296 (Arras, which included 137, the gold medallion commemorating the arrival of Constantius's fleet and army at London).

The Arras hoard also illustrates how other objects were presented in a similar way, and represented an important element of the monetary system of the late empire. The silver candlestick in the hoard was probably not just an object of personal wealth, but a present from the emperor. Many other similarly precious objects were made for imperial distribution, and their range can be seen from the page in the *Notitia Dignitatum* illustrating the post of the *comes sacrarum largitionum*, the Count of the Imperial Largesses, or official in charge of coin production (*see* Plate 21). As well as coins and bags of coins, there were gold belt buckles, leaves and precious metal bowls. Similar objects are illustrated on the back of the reverse of a gold multiple coin produced for Constantius II at Antioch, on which we can see a bag of coins between cross-bow brooches, golden leaves, golden crowns and gold rings or bracelets (157). Additionally, silver objects, such as finely worked plate, were presented on imperial anniversaries, while even silver bullion was also important: from at least 361, if not earlier, every soldier received as a gift on the accession of a new emperor five gold solidi and a pound of silver. Pieces of bullion of this sort, weighing about a pound, have been found with a hoard of solidi from Water Newton, in Cambridgeshire (Plate 20).

The monetary system of Diocletian had the effect of producing a uniform coinage from a number of mints throughout the empire (*see* Fig. 7.3). In the half century before Diocletian's reform, a number of mints had been established, as has been seen, some becoming permanent foundations and some being rather more temporary. Most of these mints seem to have been opened to meet specific needs, but Diocletian overhauled the network of existing mints (eight at his accession), and established a more logical system for them. By closing some mints (for example, Tripolis) and opening others (first, Trier and Heraclea, and, later, Aquileia, Carthage, Serdica and Nicomedia), he increased the total number to about fourteen and rationalised their location, incidentally introducing a clearer system of mint-marks to identify the products of the different mints to replace the rather chaotic marks of previous decades. As a result a rough correlation was established between mints and dioceses, the different administrative units into which the empire was organised. One should not, however, exaggerate this correlation: some areas, such as Spain, had no mint, while others, such as Gaul or Italy, had two. Other factors must also have been influential, and the distribution of mints shows an equally clear bias in favour of the area which had the heaviest concentrations of soldiers, for example the Rhine and Danube frontier regions.

FIG. 7.3 *Mints and Dioceses under Diocletian*

While Diocletian's reorganisation set the pattern for the subsequent coinage of the fourth century, the new coins – apart from the gold – which he introduced were no more successful than those of his predecessor Aurelian, in fact rather less so. The failure of the silver coinage has already been described, and the base metal coinage fared little better. It appeared to remain stable for over a decade to the extent that the physical appearance of the coins did not alter very much, but we know from the Aphrodisias inscription that the face value of the coins was doubled to give them a "geminata potentia"; it may be that this change was at least partially marked on the coinage by the appearance at some mints of the new reverse design MONETA SACRA in place of the previous GENIO POPVLI ROMANI.

Yet even in outward appearance the stability of the new system quickly became more apparent than real. The coinage suffered a series of debasements in 307, 310/11, and 313, falling in weight from 10 grams (32 to the Roman pound), to 6.8 grams (48 to the pound), to 4.5 grams (72 to the pound) and finally to about 3.4 grams (96 to the pound: for example **143**, the successor of **136**). At the same time the proportion of silver fell away from the theoretical 5% to about 1%. Despite these changes, the behaviour of the coins in hoards and the retention of basically the same designs, though with considerable variation, entitles us to regard the period from 294 to 318 as a single monetary period. Whatever the face value of the nummus became in 301, it was probably retained through the rest of the period. Rather than repeat the raising of the coin's face value while leaving the coin physically unaltered, however, the opposite tactic was adopted, and the weight and fineness of the coinage was reduced to enable a greater number of coins with the same face value to be produced from the same stock of metal, since this greater quantity was needed as a result of the sharp increase in prices.

Base metal coinage: AD 318 to 348

The year 318, however, marked the introduction of a new system, brought about, perhaps, partly in response to Licinius's reform in the east (**144**: *see* chapter six) and partly since the debasements of the system in the west had brought it to the point of collapse. The designs used on the coins changed, and hoards show a virtually complete break at this date: it seems that nearly all coins struck before 318 were demonetised and replaced by new ones. This change is entirely typical of the pattern of coinage in the fourth century. The century can be divided up into a number of similar periods. As described in chapter six, each period began with the introduction of a new coin or coins, frequently much larger and more impressive to instil confidence in their use. The introduction would usually be associated with the withdrawal of earlier coinage, but the new coinage was not generally any more successful and its inauguration was nearly always followed by debasement of its size, weight and silver content, until the whole cycle began again. This is something of an oversimplification, as at some stage in each period the heaviest or most silvery coins could be demonetised and replaced by closely related but more base successors, without a wholesale reform. Such a withdrawal affected, for instance, the two heaviest weights of the nummus in the period 294–318, as these generally do not occur in hoards of the end of the period.

The next period ran from 318–348. At its inception it was marked by the production of coins with a rather higher silver content (about 5%). Every few years the fineness and/or the weight of the coins was dropped, this change usually being marked by a new design. For instance the design of two soldiers holding two military standards with the legend GLORIA EXERCITVS (**146**) was introduced in 330 for a coin of 2.5 grams and a fineness of 1%, but when the weight was dropped to 1.7 grams in about 335 the design was altered so that the two soldiers held only one standard between them (**147**). The full range of debasement was (slightly simplified):

318–20 VICTORIAE LAETAE (**145**)	3 grams	5%
320–24 BEATA and VOTA	3 grams	2%
324–30 PROVIDENTIAE	3 grams	2%
330–35 GLORIA (2 standards: **146**)	2.5 grams	2%
335–41 GLORIA (1 standard: **147**)	1.7 grams	1%
341–48 TWO VICTORIES	1.7 grams	0%

This period, from 318–348, was also marked by a partial break in about 330, after which date it became unusual for earlier coins to remain in circulation, yet the whole period does seem to be a single one, characterised, like its predecessor, by the attempt to maintain the production of a coin with the same face value. What this value was is uncertain, but it seems possible that the coinage of 318 onwards was in some sense supposed to be the successor to the ill-fated Diocletianic silver coinage, and so perhaps valued at 100 denarii. If so, this might provide an explanation for the coin name *centenionales communes* or "common hundreders", which is known to have been applied to coins before 354; the debased silver of the 320s and 330s has been suggested as the coin in question, but the identification is not very certain.

Base metal coinage: AD 348–365

Perhaps the most ambitious reform took place at the beginning of the next period in 348, when a series of new denominations was introduced, all linked by the use of the same legend, FEL TEMP REPARATIO ("the restoration of successful times"). The three denominations were:

a 5.3 grams and about 2.5% silver (151–52)
b 4.3 grams and about 1.5% silver
c 2.4 grams and no silver (153)

This reform was no more successful than its predecessors. The production of the two smaller denominations did not last long, and the quality of the largest rapidly declined: its weight was down to about 4.4 grams in 351, to 2.5 grams in about 354 (154) and to 2.3 grams in 357.

We have simply no idea of the face value of these coins, or even of their relationship to each other, although we may be confident that a and b were much more valuable than c in view of their silver content (although this was small in quantity, it was reasonably large in value as silver was about a hundred times more valuable than copper). Yet they were certainly very highly overvalued, as had been the earlier GLORIA EXERCITVS coinage, to judge from the large numbers of imitations which were made by contemporary forgers, sensing a good profit (155, a forgery of 154). Initially, these forgeries of the FEL TEMP coinage seem to have taken the form of extracting the silver from genuine coins and then making silverless forgeries. This is perhaps what we should understand as the object of a law passed in 349:

"We [i.e. the emperors] have learned that some metalworkers (flatuarii) are purifying the larger coin (maiorina pecunia) frequently and criminally, by separating the silver from the copper. If any person be caught in this operation, let him know that he is to suffer capital punishment, and also those who own the house or land that they are to be punished by the confiscation of their property by the Treasury" (CTh 9.21.6).

Forgeries of this sort were made in appreciable numbers, but nothing like the quantity that was produced in the wave of forgery that swept the western, and to a lesser extent the eastern, empire in the 350s (155), apparently prompted by the vacuum in circulation caused by a decision taken in about 354 to demonetise earlier coins. The evidence for this demonetisation depends on the contents of hoards which show the disappearance of earlier coins, and on the fact that many of the forgeries were struck over earlier coins, implying that they were worthless. Evidence for the demonetisation is sometimes also seen in a law preserved in the Theodosian Code, whose interpretation is very much debated (*CTh* 9.23.1). This law was probably passed in 354, and makes various provisions. It re-enacted the prohibition of 349 against melting down the coins for profit, and added a similar ban on those who exported them from one province to another for profit (no doubt based on different rates for gold in different areas).

"it shall be altogether illegal for any person to buy coin (pecunias) or to handle forbidden (vetitas) coin, because legal tender ought to be money, not merchandise (quia in uso publico constitutas [pecunias] pretium oportet esse, non mercem) . . . And if ships should come to any province with goods, everything should be sold with the customary freedom except the coins which are usually called "largers" or "common hundreders" or the other ones which are known to be illegal (praeter pecunias quas more solito maiorinas vel centenionales communes appellant vel ceteras quas vetitas esse cognoscunt)

It is sometimes thought that the phrase "known to be illegal" applies to the words "maiorinas vel centenionales communes" as well as "other coins". In this way the law can be interpreted as referring to the demonetisation of the coinage of the 320s and 330s (= "centenionales") and of the finest FEL TEMP REPARATIO coins of denomination *a* (= "maiorinas"), as well as of the other illegal coins, perhaps those of the illegal usurper Magnentius (**150**). This interpretation does not, however, seem certain, as the most natural reading of the law sees it as legislating against currency speculation, whether in legal tender (maiorinae or centenionales) or illegal tender (unspecified, possibly including coins of Magnentius or possibly the earlier coins of the 320s and 330s). It is therefore not clear what exactly it has to do with the demonetisation of earlier coins and the contemporary production of imitations.

Valentinian's reform of the gold coinage

The vast number of these imitations, however, do not seem to have been removed from circulation until the 360s, perhaps in conjunction with a similarly unsuccessful reform by Julian (AD 361–63; **158**). From about this date, however, the whole monetary system began to alter, although the changes which occurred were not all connected and were introduced gradually over a period of about ten years. First in importance was the gold coinage, which was reformed in 365–68. This reform was probably prompted by concern about the quality of the gold being collected for the government in tax. Modern analyses have shown that the gold of the preceding period was debased by the addition of an increasing amount of silver, up to 5% (see Fig. 7.1), thus perhaps prompting the forgeries of gold coins of the late 350s, plated on bronze and presumably of base gold. To judge from their not uncommon survival today, such forgeries must have been made in large numbers. Moreover treasury officials are known to have substituted forgeries for genuine coins after these had been collected and before they reached the treasury (CTh 12.6.12 and 13, of 366 and 367). To alleviate this problem, it was enacted that tax payments had to be melted down and transported in bullion rather than coin, since it was simpler to test bullion. The bullion was then to be transferred as quickly as possible (within ten days, according to CTh 10.24.3 of 381) to the central treasury at the emperor's residence (comitatus), where it could be struck into new solidi by the "manufacturers of solidi" (aurifices solidorum), who were part of one of the sub-departments of the Imperial Treasury.

These new provisions had several practical effects. The melting down and reminting of solidi would have accelerated the tendency of fourth-century gold to remain in circulation for only a short time: we can see from hoards, for instance, that most of the gold in circulation was relatively newly minted. Secondly, the purity of the gold coinage was restored, and this was reflected on the coins by the addition to the mint-mark of the letters OB (159), standing for obryza or obryziacum aurum (refined gold). Thirdly, bars of gold bullion were produced from the solidi. A number of these have survived (160), bearing stamps referring to the current emperors, the name (and sometimes badge) of the provincial treasury where the coins were melted into bars, and the name of the official responsible for testing: a recent discovery shows that he was an official from the central treasury, since the name of the same man, Calliopius, has been found at two provincial treasuries, Thessalonica and Naissus. The most fundamental change which took place was, however, the establishment of the "comitatensian mint", the system whereby the minting of gold coinage was confined to the comitatus, the place of residence of the emperor, and the widespread minting of gold at other mints was curtailed; hence the abbreviation COM as part of the mint-mark of the coins from this date (165). This reform was to last to the end of the empire, and from the late 360s the production of gold was linked to the emperor's presence. This did not, of course, mean that minting was confined to a single location, since the mint, or at least part of it, could move around with the emperor. The gold bullion itself obviously moved, but so at least did some of the minting equipment, as we can infer from the die-links between different mints which are known in the fifth century. A consequence was the separation of at least some of the precious metal from the base metal minting operations: for instance in fifth-century Ravenna gold and bronze were produced in physically and administratively separate mints.

Silver coinage in the late fourth century

A somewhat similar reform affected the coinage of pure silver. Diocletian's silver coinage had not been successful, but in the reign of Constantine (306–37) a silver coinage of several denominations was revived, although only on a very small scale and perhaps only for imperial gifts on ceremonial occasions. These coins do not appear to have played any significant part in the money generally in circulation. In about 355, however, Constantius II started to produce a large quantity of silver coins, generally known today (once again without any real foundation) as *siliquae*. This large-scale production of fine silver was continued by his successors and lasted through the rest of the fourth century until it suddenly declined in about 400. The scale of the coinage can be measured from the large number of hoards which have survived, particularly in frontier areas like Britain and Romania, and from the fact that such coins are regularly found as chance losses in excavations. This implies a very large circulation.

Exactly why this coinage, unlike its predecessors, was so successful (and indeed why it was discontinued in about 400) is somewhat unclear. The reason may have something to do with its face value, although this presents something of a dilemma. If its face value was fixed artificially, then it is hard to see why it did not suffer the same fate as Diocletian's silver coin, if it is correct to think that his coin had been driven out of circulation by inflation. But if, on the other hand, it was like gold and had a free value equivalent to its bullion price, then one would have thought that changes in the relative value of gold and silver bullion would have caused endless complications for the relationship between the coins of the two metals. Perhaps it was in fact linked to gold, but with a small premium or overvaluation to cater for such fluctuations. A formal link with gold would seem to be the most obvious reason for its success, particularly in the light of the similar treatment which both it and the gold underwent in the reform of the 360s. Although the minting of silver was not confined to the emperor's presence, its fineness too was the object of imperial concern, and, at just the same time that the gold acquired the letters OB, the silver acquired the analagous PS, for *pusulatum* or "purified" (**161**). The similar treatment of the two metals in this way may perhaps support the idea that they were similarly regarded in other ways. The only other alternative to linking the face and bullion value of the silver seems to be to imagine that the government gave the coins a value which was frequently changed in response to the inflation. This seems, however, unlikely; we know, for instance, that the government improved the rates for moneychangers buying gold solidi for bronze only after complaints had been received and after the official rate had fallen behind the market rate (Symmachus, *Rel.* 29), whereas this system would have required constant anticipatory increases.

Bronze coinage in the late fourth century

The existence of a successful silver coinage also seems to have had consequences for the base metal coinage, as it seems that from the time of the successful introduction of silver coinage in about 355, debased silver was virtually discontinued and replaced by copper coinage. This is not to say that debased silver was not minted, since it was in appreciable quantities in the reform of Julian (AD 361–3: **158**) and rather more rarely by his successors Jovian and Valentinian I. The rôle of the base silver coin, however, in making up the bulk of the low value circulating medium was entirely taken over by copper coinage. It seems too that the circulation of such debased silver coins as remained was not without problems, and that they were perhaps removed from circulation in 371:

"Not only shall the bronze called dichoneutum be immediately delivered to the treasury, but it shall be entirely withdrawn from use and circulation and nobody shall be allowed to possess it publicly" (*CTh* 11.21.1, of 371).

The precise meaning of the words "aes dichoneutum" is obscure, but it seems reasonable to suppose that it means "alloyed" and probably refers to the base silver coins of Julian and his successors. Apart from these rare large denominations, the low value currency of the next fifteen years from 364 to about 379 was almost entirely composed of copper coins of about 2.5 grams (GLORIA ROMANORVM and SECVRITAS REIPVBLICAE: **162**). In about

379, however, Gratian introduced a larger coin of about 5.3 grams (**163**) and a smaller one of about 1.5 grams, while continuing the issue of the 2.5 gram coin. The legend of the largest coin, REPARATIO REIPVB (**163**): "the restoration of the state") and its weight standard seem to echo that of the same denomination of 348; these coins, however, contained no silver, although we have no idea of their relationship with the other two denominations.

The monetary history of the last years of the fourth century is not at all clear. The reform of 379, instigated by Gratian, lasted for a few years, although production of the intermediate denomination was soon stopped and that of the largest denomination was discontinued after some five years. Thereafter, in the western half of the empire, base metal coinage was virtually confined to the production of the smallest denomination; initially this had been characterised by a design referring to imperial anniversaries (vota), but from 388 its weight was again lowered to just over 1 gram and the design replaced with that of a figure of Victory holding a wreath and a palm (**166–67**). In the east, Gratian's system was replaced in about 383 by a new system of Theodosius I, whose main difference was an increase in weight of the largest denomination; as in the west, however, it was the smallest denomination that was produced in the greatest numbers. Both design and weight standard were much the same in east and west, and hoards show a predominance of these coins (rather than the other, larger denominations), which clearly formed the bulk of the currency down to about 400. It may be that all the larger denominations then in existence were demonetised by a law in 395:

"We command that only the centenionalis nummus shall be handled in public use, the making of the larger coin (maior pecunia) having been discontinued. No persons, therefore, shall dare to exchange the decargyrus nummus (the "tenner coin"?) for another coin, knowing that it will be confiscated by the treasury if found in public use" (*CTh* 9.23.2, of 395).

Larger coins did, however, continue to be made in very small quantities, although the largest size was exceptionally rare, and was only minted in the middle of the century at Constantinople. Issues of the intermediate size, at a weight of about 2.2 grams, continued to be made in the west at Rome until about 410, and in the east at a number of mints until about 425. Thereafter bronze coinage was effectively confined to the smallest denomination, whose minting continued until the end of the fifth century.

The survey of the monetary history of the late empire given in this chapter has of necessity been selective, due to the obvious complexity and uncertainty of the subject, particularly at the end of the century. This account has concentrated on the mainstream of the coinage, and little notice has been taken of the often very interesting coinages of usurpers like Magnentius (AD 350–53: **150**) or Procopius (AD 365–66), both of whom for instance made several short-lived innovations in the coinage. It can be seen that throughout the period the same general pattern took place: a stable gold and later a stable silver coinage was accompanied by a succession of complicated attempts to stabilise the bronze or base silver coinage, all of which rapidly ran into trouble and eventually collapsed, only tò be replaced subsequently by another attempt. The repeated failure of these attempts should perhaps be blamed on the intrinsic instability of the system, pumping more and more purely token coinage into the economy in an effort to keep up with inflation, but in fact merely exacerbating it. Stability of a sort seems to have returned in the fifth century, but it was a stability that was finally wrecked by the political disintegration of the empire in the west.

Chapter Eight

Designs: the coming of Christianity

Introduction

The choice of coin designs in the late empire was assumed by contemporaries to lie with the emperor. This is clear, not just from the description in Eusebius of how Constantine made coins of himself in an attitude of prayer (*see* chapter four), but also in a rather quaint pamphlet entitled *de rebus bellicis* (On Military Affairs), which was addressed to the emperors in the late fourth century. At the beginning of this work, the author makes various suggestions about the coinage, and recommends new designs for the gold and bronze coinage. These designs were shown in a picture of *Felix incohatio sacrae divinaeque monetae*, "A Favourable New Start for the Sacred and Divine Currency", but unfortunately the original picture seems to have been lost in the transmission of the manuscript. Nevertheless, the very fact that the author made his suggestions in this way indicates that he assumed that the designs were chosen by the emperor himself.

As in the early empire, however, the actual mechanism of choice may have been more complex, although we do not know the importance of the role of the *comes sacrarum largitionum*, "Count of Imperial Largesses", the official in charge of the one of the three main financial departments of the late empire which dealt with mints, mines, state clothing factories and the distribution of precious metal coinage to the army. Nor can we really assess the role of the man in charge of each individual mint, the *procurator Monetae*, although the general similarity of the designs used at different mints obviously implies that he cannot have had more than a fairly minor interpretative role. An examination of the details of the designs used at different mints in the 330s, for example, has made it possible to form a rough idea of how detailed a model or pattern was sent out. The differences and similarities of detail suggest that rough (perhaps only written?) instructions were sent out, specifying only the general layout of the design and the inscriptions to be used, but not such details as how the figures on the reverse should be clothed, or the sort of wreath to be used for the emperor.

The sorts of design actually used developed from those described for the third century, the banal selection of gods and personified virtues, which had been relieved only in the middle of the century by the more innovative and subtle coinages of Gallienus and Postumus. From Aurelian's reform in 274 the link between a particular design and a particular section of the mint (*see* chapter four) was dropped. As a result designs were less diverse, and tended to concentrate on only a few themes in order to propagate the power and position of the emperor more efficiently. Yet the stylised designs, which seem so foreign to us and so different from those of the early empire, were only one aspect of the formalised ritual of the late empire. This can be seen clearly from the comparison of coin designs and the topical tableaux set up officially in public places. In the fifth century we have one description of such public scenes:

"He [the prefect of the city of Rome] placed small placards in the middle of the Circus to sketch out some pictures of current affairs; by putting all sorts of absurd details in the pictures he implicitly made a mockery of the scene. He did not depict the Emperor's Bravery (andreian basileos) or the Strength of the Armies (romen stratioton) or any well known and just war, but a hand stretched out as if from the clouds with the inscription 'The hand of God driving off barbarians'. It was appalling, but necessary, to write this. And again elsewhere: 'Barbarians escaping from God'. And other things more inappropriate than these . . .' (Eunapius fr. 78).

The Emperor's Bravery or the Strength of the Armies were typical subjects for late imperial coin design, as the frequent occurrence of designs like VIRTVS AVGVSTI or VIRTVS MILITVM makes clear; thus we can see that the language of coin designs was the same as that of other forms of imperial "propaganda".

Gods, emperors and portraits

The designs used during the late third century were obsessed with the military security of the empire and the emperor's allegedly crucial role in maintaining it. The slogans PAX and VICTORIA, peace or victory, are constant themes, inversely and sharply reflecting the severe military pressures on the empire at this time. The importance of the emperor's military role as RESTITVTOR ORBIS ("Restorer of the World") was reflected in the increasing use of warlike portraits, showing the emperor wearing a helmet or holding weapons (**128**, of Probus). His powers to resist the constant threats to the security of the empire were emphasised on the reverses of his coins, for instance his own

VIRTVS or natural bravery (**128**), or PROVIDENTIA, foresight. There was a strong emphasis on the divine protection which aided his military prowess and therefore that of the empire. In the reign of Gallienus the mint of Rome had produced a series of coins commemorating the gods whose protection Gallienus claimed. so-and-so CONS(ervator) AVG(usti). Gallienus put most emphasis on Diana (**120**), but he also claimed the protection of Hercules, whose help was heavily stressed by his rival the Gallic usurper Postumus (**121**). Hercules and particularly the Sun-god, Sol (**126**, of Aurelian), were the dominant divine protectors of the emperor on the coinage of the later third century, as they were pre-eminently the gods of Victory: Sol was *invictus* or unconquered, while Hercules was the pacifier (HERC PACIFERO). This emphasis led to the emperor being likened to and practically identified with the gods in question: Gallienus's and Postumus's portraits (**121**) were occasionally depicted with Hercules's lionskin or club, while the emperors like Aurelian (AD 270–75) and Probus (AD 276–82) were closely likened to Sol. The most remarkable, though rare, instances of this come from the Balkan mints of Siscia and Serdica, where there were a series of explicit legends for several emperors, from Aurelian to Carus, describing each of them as DEO ET DOMINO, "God and Lord"; in one case Carus is shown with Sol with the legend, DEO ET DOMINO CARO INVIC AVG "to the god and lord Carus, the unconquered emperor". Similarly, on a medallion made at Rome for Probus, the emperor is depicted together with the radiate head of Sol, and his titles include that of Sol, INVICTVS (**129**). It was now standard for the emperor to be, like Sol, *invictus*.

With his establishment of the tetrarchic system, whereby the empire was divided between four emperors, Diocletian (284–305) formalised a detailed relationship between the emperors and different gods to reflect the different relative status of each emperor. The two senior were respectively presented as the son of Jupiter (**131** for Diocletian) and of Hercules (**132**, for his colleague Maximian), and the two junior each as a son of one of the seniors in a sort of divine family, even though all were unrelated. The choice of Jupiter for Diocletian is a little unexpected, given the preference of most of his successors for Sol. Jupiter had also been a protector of Probus and Carinus, but this role was not given anything like the prominence which Diocletian accorded to it. Diocletian may have preferred him because, as the chief god, his position was more appropriate to the emperor; or he may have preferred to use one of the traditional Roman gods, rather than one of the newer oriental cults like that of Sol. The subsequent adoption of Hercules as his colleague Maximian's protector was probably prompted both by the recent use of Hercules as an imperial protector, and by the fact that Hercules was Jupiter's son. The imagery was picked up, for instance, by the anonymous author of a speech written in praise of Maximian in 289: "Jupiter rules heaven and Hercules pacifies the earth; just as in all great enterprises it is Diocletian who directs them and you who carry them out" (*Pan.* 2(10).11.6).

Despite his formalisation of the system of divine family, it is ironic that Diocletian, in his coinage reform, directed attention away from the different statuses of the emperors and more towards the idea of the empire. The portraits of the emperors were starkly insensitive heads, hardly differentiated from each other at all, and without any of the special warlike or other representations which had become relatively common in the preceding decades (**134–36**). Gone too were the ways of denoting rank by the use of different bust types. The senior emperor had previously been shown wearing a cloak and seen from the rear (**131**), the second most important wearing armour (**132**), and more junior colleagues wearing cloaks and seen from in front (**133**). All were now shown with unadorned and simple portrait heads, with no indications of status (e.g. **136**). The reverses too, at any rate of the silver and base silver, became standardised and uniform, dwelling in the case of silver on military themes (**135**) and in the case of the base silver nummus on the Spirit of the Roman People, GENIO POPVLI ROMANI (**136**): for the first time in the third century a design was used which was the same at all mints and yet which did not refer to the emperor. Thus the impression conveyed by Diocletian's new coinage was of an empire securely united under the depersonalised power of the tetrarchic system.

It is perhaps not surprising that this uniformity did not outlast the stability of Diocletian's imperial system, and the series of civil wars which lasted from 306 to 324 prompted a new wave of innovation. The emphasis shifted back from the state as a whole to the individual ruler: GENIO POPVLI ROMANI was replaced, for instance, by GENIO AVGVSTI. Imperial claimants stressed their own appeals for support: Maxentius in Rome recalled the old glory of Rome (for example **138**, using the old symbol of the wolf and twins: compare **8**), while the emergent Constantine stressed his descent from Constantius, one of the original tetrarchs; hence also his unbearded portrait, to signify his position as the young son of Constantius. Initially Constantine also claimed the divine protection of Mars. His Mars phase, however, was superseded in

310 with a vision in which Apollo-Sol appeared to him with omens of success (Pan. 7(6).21), and thereafter his coinage was dominated for several years by "his companion, the unconquered Sol", SOLI INVICTO COMITI (**139**). With Constantine's eventual victory in 324, however, several changes came over the coinage. First the brutal tetrarchic portrait was replaced by Constantine's more bland and unbearded portrait (**139**), a classical portrait which had begun much earlier and spread, like the weight of the new solidus, from west to east with Constatine's victories. Subsequent emperors copied this image for their "portraits" (**151**) to stress the legitimacy, whether real or usurped, of their succession from Constantine: hence the frequent problems of identifying late Roman sculptures or even of distinguishing on coins between emperors with the same name like Constantine and his son Constantine II. Individualised portraits did occur later, but only as the rare choice made by a usurper, such as Magnentius (AD 350–53: **150**), to stress his difference from the existing regime. Thereafter all portraits were more or less identical; the only exception was the beard worn by Julian as a badge of his paganism (**158**). The beard was also adopted as part of the official portrait of the later usurpers Eugenius (AD 392–94: **165**) and Johannes (AD 423–35) perhaps to increase their appeal to pagans; for the same reason other emperors, like Honorius, who had beards in real life did not normally use them on their official image.

The second change which came over the appearance of the coinage with Constantine's victory and the end of civil war was the return to the less specific and less value-laden reverse designs, such as the "Glory of the Army", GLORIA EXERCITVS (**146–7**) or the "Safety of the State", SECVRITAS REIPVBLICAE (**162**). The reason for the particular choice is not usually obvious, as some of them seem to have little specific point, except, as we saw in chapter seven, to denote a change in the physical properties of the coinage. An exception was, however, the coinage inaugurated in 348 to mark the 1100th anniversary of the city of Rome. Several different designs were chosen in a programmatic scheme, all linked by the use of a single legend, FEL TEMP REPARATIO, "The Restoration of Successful Times". The phoenix, symbol of renewal, appears on one denomination (**153**): the renewal of the fortunes of the empire is warranted by the military successes of the emperors depicted on the other denominations, such as Constans's expedition to Britain (the emperor on galley design: **151**) and Constantius's victory over the Persians (the emperor spearing a fallen horseman: **152**). The unified concep-

144

tion of the FEL TEMP coinage makes it stand out from the normally bland and repetitive fourth-century designs. As with portraits, however, the coinage of usurpers could break this neutrality, to promote the usurper's special claims to rule. One of the most famous of these was the large chi-rho symbol, used by Magnentius towards the end of his reign (**150**) to stress his Christianity and his claim to be the successor of Constantine, perhaps taking advantage of opposition to the support given by the legitimate emperor Constantius II to Arianism (one of Arianism's great opponents, Paul of Constantinople, was supposed to have been in correspondence with Magnentius). Similarly, Vetranio in 350 had put on the coins that he minted in his own name and that of Constantius a more detailed version of the famous vision of Constantine before the Battle of the Milvian Bridge in 312: the emperor holds a banner with a chi-rho and is crowned by Victory, together with the legend HOC SIGNO VICTOR ERIS, "Under this sign you will be victor" (**149**). In this way he stressed the position of himself and Constantius, rather than Magnentius, as the true successors of Constantine.

Christianity

The designs used by Magnentius and Vetranio introduce the third important aspect of the coinage of Constantine, namely the extent to which it reflected his conversion to Christianity. There was, however, no sudden shift from pagan to Christian imagery. This need not perhaps surprise us too much, as there was at the time no official Christian iconography to draw on. Pagan gods such as Sol only disappeared from Constantine's coinage in 318, six years after his conversion, and even then their disappearance seems to have been prompted more by the desire to reform the monetary system (*see* chapter seven), than to change its iconography. The new types which replaced it were, however, not specifically Christian, but neutral representations of soldiers or personifications like Victory. The only explicitly Christian coin designs were the representation of the emperor in the attitude of prayer (**140**), and the very rare design used at the mint of Constantinople in about 327, showing a banner with a chi-rho monogram spearing a serpent, representing his enemy Licinius (**142**). The chi-rho monogram was, because of Constantine's vision of 312, the most important symbol of his Christianity, but its appearance on coins of his reign was largely confined to its use as one of the stock of symbols used for mint-marks. Thus its use at most would seem to reflect the predeliction of the procurator

Monetae of, for instance, Arles in about 332 or Antioch in about 336, rather than resulting from any more central decision. The symbol appeared rather more systematically as part of the mint-mark at the mints of Ticinum Aquileia, Siscia and Thessalonica in about 320, where the contemporaneity of its appearance and the similarly odd way the monogram was drawn make one feel that there was some single inspiration, although it is difficult to see what this might have been as the mints were in three different dioceses. These examples then serve to illustrate the choice only of some official or officials, and result from the new atmosphere of official Christianity and the new presence of Christians in the imperial administration. Like the Christian designs, however, they are all very rare, and do not give much sign that the official iconography of the emperor was very much influenced by Christianity.

In this respect, however, something of a controversy surrounds the appearance of a chi-rho on the helmet worn by Constantine on a silver medallion minted at Rome or Aquileia in 315 (**141**) or on some bronze coins of Siscia of about 320 (**145**). Are these to be seen as evidence that Constantine now used the chi-rho as part of his official representation, or are they to be interpreted as only casual appearances reflecting some local official's choice, along the same lines as the occasional appearance of the symbol in mint-marks? It is indeed hard to disassociate them from Eusebius's explicit statement (3.2) that Constantine placed the chi-rho on his helmet, but the very occasional nature of its appearance on coins should make us cautious of making too much of this. On coins minted in about 322 at Trier, for instance, the chi-rho appeared as the decoration on the shield held by Constantine's son Crispus; but it happened on only one die and must represent the personal choice of a die engraver, as other dies for the same group of coins have different sorts of decoration on the shield.

After his death in 337, Constantine was deified, like many of his pagan predecessors, but the iconography of his apotheosis was Christianised. Previous emperors had ridden up to heaven on a chariot; Constantine was received by the *manus dei* (**148**): the design was described by Eusebius in the passage quoted in chapter four. The "hand of God" was, with the chi-rho monogram, one of the most important Christian symbols to appear on the coinage of the late empire. Its use was gradually developed, and from the late fourth century it was sometimes shown holding a wreath over the head of an emperor or empress, becoming specifically associated with the appointment of new emperors, as can be seen, for instance, on the accession solidi of young Valentinian III in 425 (**169**); whereas the pagan emperor had been selected by the gods (*princeps a diis electus*), the Christian was chosen, and crowned, by God. In such ways Christian symbols came to play a part in the iconography of the emperor and the empire. From 443, the personification of the city of Constantinople was regularly shown holding a cross; previously she had held only a sceptre or a globe. Another clear example is provided by the rare coins which show the emperor as consul and which were probably minted for distribution by the emperor at the consular games over which he presided. They illustrate how the traditional regalia of that ancient magistracy were gradually Christianised, since the plain or eagle tipped sceptre was replaced from 422 by a sceptre with a cross (**172**), which thereafter remained standard.

At about the same time, Christianity came to play a more dominant role on the coinage. Generally speaking, in the fourth century Christian symbols received less prominence than in the fifth. Even from the mid fourth century, when the emperor was often shown holding a banner with the chi-rho monogram, Christian designs in no way dominated the coinage. Other designs still formed the majority: personifications like Victory and Hope or the often repeated GLORIA ROMANORVM, references to actual events, such as Constans's visit to Britain and, particularly on the gold coinage, references to imperial anniversaries (*vota*: **156** for Constantius II), no doubt reflecting the important of the cash presents of 5 solidi each given to the soldiers on these occasions. Apart from the exceptional coinage of Magnentius, however, it was only in the fifth century that a chi-rho or a cross formed the whole or part of the design of a coin, for instance on the bronze coins of Theodosius II (402–50) or on the silver of his wife Eudocia.

East and west

In 395 Theodosius I had died, and the empire was divided between his sons Honorius, ruling the west from Ravenna, and Arcadius, ruling the east from Constantinople. One of the results of this division was the use of different coin designs in each half. Although the division between west and east was formalised in 395, it had already previously become apparent on the coinage. Western solidi had tended to have a representation of two emperors with a figure of Victory (**165**), while in the east the personification of Constantinople was normal, as, for instance, on coins of Theodosius (**164**). Western silver had tended to have the personification of Rome, whereas eastern silver usually referred to vota. From 395 on, however, the designs used in the different parts of the empire were almost completely different. This was most apparent on the obverse, which symbolised the division of the empire, since western solidi continued to use the traditional profile bust of the emperor (**170**), whereas in the east he was portrayed helmeted and three-quarters facing (**173**). When, exceptionally, a western emperor like Anthemius used a facing and helmeted image, this can be explained by the fact that he was an eastern nominee for the western throne.

The reverses also differed after 395. The standard design on the reverse of eastern solidi of the fifth century was the cross with the figure of Victory (**172–3**: the "auream monetam cum signo crucis" of St. Prosper *de prom.* 2.34). This was originally perhaps a symbol of the triumph achieved by the Christian emperor Theodosius II with his victory in 421 over the Persians, and was introduced onto the coinage in 422 (**172**). In the west, the design of the emperor with a captive was replaced, from 425, by the emperor standing on a human-headed serpent (**170**), presumably a reference to the defeat of the usurper Johannes (AD 423–25). This design continued to be used for most of the rest of the period of the western empire. Its inapplicability after the end of the reign of Valentinian III, who had replaced Johannes, underlines how coin designs tended to become ossified during the period. With the revival of the cross and victory designs by Marcian in 450 (**173**), the type used on eastern solidi was almost as static, as were the designs used on tremisses or thirds of the solidus. The clearest indication of this immobilisation, however, can be seen in the design used on gold half-solidi or semisses. For Theodosius II's thirty-fifth anniversary, the design was a figure of Victory inscribing xxxv on a shield, but this design became standard for his subsequent semisses and those of other emperors despite its inappropriateness (e.g. **174**, of Marcian).

The divergence of coin designs in east and west had directly symbolised the division of the empire; the immobilisation of designs during the fifth century is an inverse symbol of the crisis which suddenly beset the empire, the violent incursions of germanic tribes, which swept through the empire, sacking Rome, weakening its emperors and bringing about its final collapse. The unchanging nature of coin designs at the time stands out, like the eternal youthfulness of Augustus's portrait five centuries before, as a vision of permanency. In this case, however, the vision was blind.

PART FOUR

Chapter Nine

From Rome to the medieval world

The monetary system of the fifth century

In the fifth century the many different denominations of the previous century petered out, resulting in a much simpler monetary system. At the same time the tendency, noted on the coinage from the 380s, for the western and eastern halves of the empire to behave independently both in terms of design and denominations became formalised in 395 with the death of Theodosius I and the division of the empire between his young sons Arcadius, ruling the east from Constantinople, and Honorius, ruling the west from Ravenna. From the time of the feeble Honorius, however, the western emperors were for the most part mere puppets of the Commander of the Army (Magister Militum). It was they, men like Stilicho, Aetius and Ricimer, who wielded real power and who appointed a succession of emperors until power was taken by Odovacar, who decided to dispense with a western emperor altogether. In the east, the generals did not acquire such power, and, after the deposition of the last western emperor in 476, the eastern emperors continued to rule as "Byzantine" emperors for another thousand years. Despite the de facto division of the empire, the two halves remained in theory a unity. Laws were headed by the names of the current rulers of both parts of the empire, and coins issued by any emperor were legal tender throughout the empire. Moreover, a mint, whether it was in the east or the west, would usually strike coins in the names of all the current emperors.

The number of mints operating had been greatly reduced from the fourteen of Diocletian as a result of the monetary reforms and political changes of the late fourth and early fifth centuries. The production of gold had been centralised with the division between the base metal coinage produced at separate State Mints (Monetae Publicae) and the precious metal coinage produced at the comitatensian mint under the direct control of

149

the comes sacrarum largitionum. In practice this meant that gold in the fifth century was coined at only one mint in each part of the empire, normally the imperial residences of Ravenna (**170**, with the mint-mark RV) and Constantinople (**172**, with the mint-mark CON). In the east, however, a regular, but very small, gold coinage was also produced at Thessalonica, while in the west, from the middle of the century, the mint of Milan produced an important gold coinage, apparently under the control of the Magister Militum. Bronze, on the other hand, was produced elsewhere. In the west it was confined to the mint of Rome (**168**), which had a vast output, although occasionally small issues were also made elsewhere at the beginning of the century, e.g. in Gaul for Honorius and Theodosius II. In the east, although Constantinople was the principal mint for bronze (**176**) as well as gold, several other mints (Thessalonica, Heraclea, Nicomedia, Cyzicus, Antioch and Alexandria), continued to produce bronze down to the time of Leo (457–74) and Zeno (474–91), though not in very large quantities.

The most important coins were in gold, the solidus and its third or tremissis (**171**), a denomination which had been introduced in 383 by Theodosius and which came to play an increasingly important role in the fifth century. As noted in chapter eight, the designs for these coins reflected the division of the empire. On solidi in the west, the emperor's portrait followed previous practice and was normally shown in profile (**170**), whereas in the east he was usually shown almost facing, wearing a helmet and holding a spear and a shield (**173**). The reverses also varied. The predominant design on western solidi showed the emperor holding a long cross and trampling down a human-headed serpent (**170**), while in the east the usual design was a long cross supported by a figure of Victory (**172–3**). Tremisses in both west and east used profile portraits, but in the west the reverse usually had a cross in wreath (**171**) and in the east a facing figure of Victory.

After the demise of the plentiful silver coinage of the late fourth century, silver was minted in only very small quantities, despite a partial revival in the reign of Leo (it became plentiful again only in the seventh century under Heraclius and Constans II). The bronze coinage was, however, still substantial. As described in chapter seven, the multi-denominational system of the fourth century survived in a restricted form into the early years of the fifth. It soon, however, died out, by about 415 in the west and some ten years later in the east. Thereafter nearly all bronzes were tiny in size, about 9 mm in diameter (less than half the size of a modern 1p coin) and weighing no more than about a gram, although even this weight was reduced during the century. These coins were extensively imitated by forgers and were produced in large numbers, since, in the absence of any substantive denomination between them and the tremissis (worth about 2,400), vast numbers were required to enable one coin to be exchanged for the other. This extremely inconvenient state of affairs demonstrates that the government's production of bronze coinage was not motivated by any consideration for the convenience of the public, but by its desire to recover as much gold as possible through the moneychangers. In the reign of Valentinian III (AD 425–55) they were required to buy solidi from the public at not less than 7000 nummi and sell them to the treasury at 7,200 (Val. *Nov.* 16). For reasons that are not entirely clear, and in contrast to the situation in the fourth century, the rate of exchange between gold and bronze coins appears to have remained fairly stable throughout the period. It is not easy to be sure of this, since there is not much evidence and since different terminology is used to describe the coins, which may be referred to as "nummi" (e.g. in the law just cited), "denarii" (e.g. in a writer like John Cassian, *Inst. Mon.* 4.4) or "myriads of denarii" in Egyptian papyri. In view of the low values involved there must have been some change in the way of reckoning since the fourth century, perhaps involving a use of "nummus" to mean 10,000 earlier denarii. And on the risky hypotheses that these terms were interchangeable and that evidence from different parts of the empire is comparable we can construct the following table of equivalences between the solidus and bronze coin:

445	7200	(Val. *Nov.* 16)
c. 493	14400	(*JRS* 1959.73)
498	?16800	(inference about Anastasian reform)
c. 512(?)	8400	(210 folles at 40 nummi (Procopius 25.11.12)
539(?)	7200	(180 folles at 40 nummi (Procopius ibid.)
6th cent	7200	(*POxy* 2195)
6th cent	7200	(*POxy* 1917)

Despite all the uncertainties in these figures, the rampant inflation of the fourth century does appear to have moderated considerably. To explain this we would perhaps have expected to find, if not a contraction of the quantity of money, at least a stabilisation of the absolute and relative quantities of gold and bronze. It is extremely difficult to demonstrate whether or not this occurred, although one must say that it does not seem very likely. One can indeed point out that the silver coinage of the late fourth century had disappeared, even though we have no way of knowing how significant a contribution it made to the stock of precious metal coinage. On the other hand, to judge from the roughly equal numbers of gold coins lost from circulation in the fourth and in the fifth centuries and recovered today as chance finds, it seems that there was as much or only slightly less gold in circulation, despite the drain of gold required for subsidies to buy protection from the barbarian peoples in the west and the Persians in the east. On the other hand these subsidies, though often quite large (for example, the Huns were paid an annual subsidy of 350 pounds of gold or 25,200 solidi from about AD 422, 700 pounds from about AD 437 and 2100 pounds from about AD 447), do not really seem to have been very substantial when compared with imperial expenditure or the state budget (perhaps of the order of some 5 million solidi per annum), and some emperors were able to accumulate large surpluses: 100,000 pounds of gold by Theodosius II and Marcian (John Lydus, *de Mag.* 3.43), or 23 million solidi, equivalent to about 320,000 pounds of gold, by Anastasius (Procopius, *Secret History* 19.7).

As for bronze coinage, there seems no good way of assessing its extent relative to the fourth century. It does not seem to be true, as has been alleged, that bronze coinage virtually ceased after the death of Theodosius I in 395, since large quantities of fifth-century bronze have survived today and there are a number of large hoards. On the other hand, it is true that, geographically, its use contracted, since fifth-century bronze circulated only in the Mediterranean parts of the Roman world. When one looks at the lists of coins found during excavations in those areas, for example at Athens, Sardis or Carthage, there does at first seem to be a relative absence of bronzes of the fifth century compared with finds of the fourth or sixth centuries, but we should remember firstly that the tiny size of the coins makes them very hard to find in excavations, and secondly that the sites always have an extremely large number of illegible pieces, most of which look as if they were minted in the fifth or early sixth century.

Thus the impression given by this evidence, which is hardly very valid statistically, is that if anything there was a small decline in the amount of precious metal in the fifth century, and at the same time that very large numbers of nummi were produced, hardly any less than previously. If this impression is correct, then its effect should have been to accelerate the inflation of the bronze coin against the gold, quite the opposite of what seems to have been the case. A possible explanation of this problem is perhaps to suppose that gold coinage had by now become the coinage of account, and that therefore prices were expressed in gold rather than some other notional unit of account, like the denarius of the fourth century. It was noted in the discussion of inflation in the fourth century (*see* chapter six) that prices in terms of gold did not appear to have risen, simply because gold was a commodity whose price would also rise in step with the general price of other commodities. But if the price of commodities were expressed in gold, then, assuming a reasonably constant quantity of gold in circulation, inflation would simply disappear. Some support for this view can be found in Egyptian papyri, which tend to express prices in fractions of the solidus, for instance fractions as small as one ninety-sixth (roughly equivalent in relative purchasing power to an early imperial dupondius), whereas there was, of course, no actual coin smaller than the third or tremissis. Similarly fifth-century laws regulating prices of foodstuffs, for example, generally talk in terms of so many pounds to a quantity of gold, rather than to so many nummi or denarii. The obvious occasion for such a change to gold is 396, when a law was passed:

"The price of bronze coin (aeris pretia) which is demanded from provincials, we wish to be exacted in such a way that for twenty-five pounds of bronze a solidus shall be given over by the possessor" (*CTh* 11.21.2).

A later law of AD 424 refers to the fixed value of bronze to gold (aurum, quod aestimatio certa constituit pro centenario aeris . .: *CTh* 11.21.3), and in view of this fixed relationship between gold and bronze we can regard the figures in the table of equivalences as representing the official fixed rate of exchange between solidi and bronze coins. This changed with the decline in the weight standard of bronzes, since the relationship was fixed by weight: a value of 7200 implies a bronze coin of 1.13 grams, while a value of 14,400 implies one of 0.56 grams, and indeed these are not far off the actual weights of the nummus in hoards before and after the weight reductions which took place in the course of the fifth century. One should not press such calculations too far, as it seems likely that the ratio between gold and bronze was changed at some time. Between the inclusion of the law of 396 in Theodosius II's codification of 434 and its re-enactment in

Justinian's law code of 534, the figure of twenty-five pounds was replaced with twenty, probably implying that this change had taken place some time before 534. But as we do not know when the change occurred, detailed calculations of coin weight are rather pointless. Finally, one might perhaps also guess that in 396 the number of bronze coins to the solidus was 6000. This would suit a coin weighing 1.35 grams (the approximate weight of the then smallest current coin) and would make sense of the remark of Cassiodorus, writing in about 510, that "the ancients wanted the solidus to be of six thousand denarii" (*sex milia denariorum solidum esse voluerunt* [sc. *veteres*]: *Var.* 1.10).

The reform of bronze

The uniformity of circulation of the small bronze nummi continued, until at the very end of the empire there was a reform introducing larger denominations. In the eastern (Byzantine) part of the empire this reform was introduced in 498 by John Caiaphas, the comes sacrarum largitionum of the emperor Anastasius (491–518). He inaugurated a coinage of larger bronze coins, marked with their value in Greek numerals, м for 40 nummi (**181**), к for 20, ι for 10 and later ε for 5; the largest denomination was called in Latin the *teruncianus* or "coin weighing one third of an ounce" and in Greek the *follaris*, more generally known as the *follis*. The motive for this reform is not recorded explicitly, but appears to have been the wish to fill the void in the monetary system between the gold tremissis and its less than thousandth part, the nummus. At any rate, Marcellinus, writing at the time, records that the reform was "pleasing to the people" (placabilem plebi: *Chronicon*, under 498).

One wonders why, if such a move was so popular, and clearly relatively easy, it was not done earlier in the preceding seventy-five years or so while the problem of the absence of small change had existed. On the face of it an attempt to provide just such a remedy had been made at Constantinople in the later fifth century, when larger bronze coins, weighing about 4.5 grams, were minted by Theodosius II, Leo (in particular: **175**) and Zeno. Yet these coins were not minted in very large quantities, and appear – to judge from finds – to have been made for some special local use in the Crimea, rather than for circulation throughout the empire. So these coins did not represent an attempt to provide the whole empire with an intermediate series of coins. Moreover, when we look at the immediate origins of Anastasius's reform it is hard to avoid the conclusion that it was ultimately prompted by an accident. The predecessors of the reform were in the late fifth century west: in Africa, now ruled by the Vandal kings who produced a series of large bronze coins, marked with their value XLII, XXI and XII (nummi), and in Italy, ruled by Odovacar (476–493), who recognised the eastern emperor Zeno. Sometime before the death of that emperor in 491, Odovacar produced a series of large bronze coins, partly in the name of Zeno (**178**) and partly commemorating IMVICTA ROMA, "Unconquered Rome", in two denominations marked XL (**179**) and XX, pieces of 40 and 20 nummi, obviously immediate prototypes of Anastasius reformed denominations. The design used on the coins minted in the name of Zeno is a figure of Victory advancing with the letters SC, highly reminiscent of bronze asses of the late first century AD, as was the shape, size and general aspect of the new coins (compare **178** with the as of Vespasian, **87**). Moreover, it seems that it was precisely at this time that a very large hoard of such early imperial bronzes, mostly of Vespasian (AD 69–79), was discovered. These coins were incised with contemporary values: LXXXIII on sestertii (**177**) and XLII on dupondii or asses. Because of the numerals it used to be thought that this discovery and revaluation took place in Vandal Africa, but nearly all the finds of these coins have been made in Italy, which anyway seems a more likely origin in view of the similarity in design between the Zeno coins of Odovacar and some such first-century bronzes. The different values (XL against XLII) may perhaps represent the difference between the official and market rates of the coins (compare chapter five); at any rate, it seems that these coins of Vespasian provided the inspiration both for Odovacar's and consequently for the Vandal and Byzantine reforms. Yet the fact that the whole series of reforms was prompted by the accidental discovery of a very large hoard of early imperial coins strongly suggests that, until the idea presented itself with the backing of antiquity, the idea of large bronze denominations, intermediate between the tremissis and the nummus, simply had not occurred or at any rate had not been taken seriously by the government.

The break-up of the empire

Thus by the end of the fifth century, the coinage we know as Byzantine had developed out of the late Roman. We should, of course, hardly have expected any immediate or particular change, since the beginning of the "Byzantine" empire represented no new political regime, merely the continuation of what

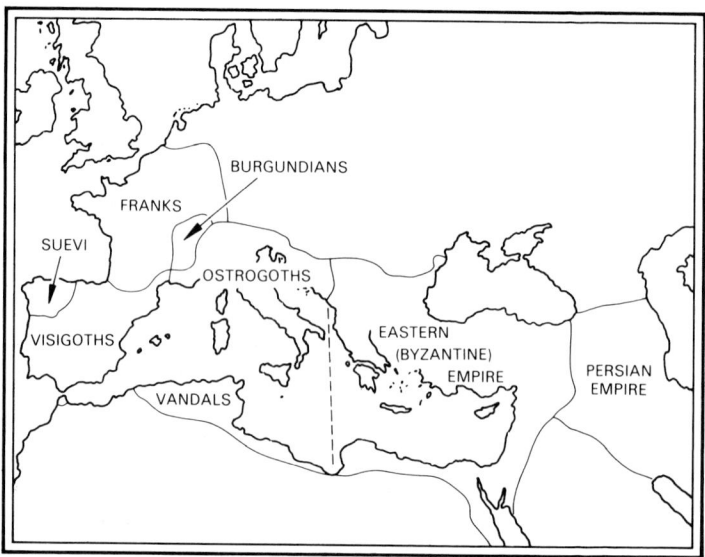

FIG. 9.1 The Break-up of the Empire

was left after the final collapse of the west. The standard reverse design of the solidus, the cross and victory, persisted with variations until the seventh century. Similarly, the iconography of the late Roman emperors made only a gradual transition to that of their "Byzantine" successors. The three-quarter facing portrait with spear and shield was altered in 538 by the emperor Justinian to a fully facing one with orb and shield. The Roman tradition of an unchanging imperial image was only broken, however, from the reign of Tiberius II (578–82), when the helmet was frequently replaced by different crowns, used to individualise the image of each different emperor. Over the same period, the regalia of the consulship, previously worn by the emperor and shown on his coins only in the years in which he held that magistracy (**172**), became part of his permanent costume. As well as continuing its iconography, the "Byzantine" coinage also took over the de-nominations of the late Roman coinage. Gold solidi and tremisses, together with very rare silver coins, were minted at the same weight standards. The bronze had, as it happens, been reformed, but only twenty years after the fall of the last western emperor and as a response to changes in the barbarian kingdoms of the west.

One can similarly overestimate the change to the monetary system that happened with the collapse of the west and its replacement by the mainly Germanic kingdoms. These barbarian tribes had no tradition of coinage. The first coins that they met were those of the late Roman empire, which they received as pay when fighting in the imperial armies or as subsidies for not attacking the empire. Consequently, it is no surprise that, when they took over the territories formerly controlled by Rome, they took over the same coins as the Romans. They used the same denominations and their coins had the same general appearance, often closely imitating imperial prototypes. Tribes outside the boundaries of the old empire do not seem to have produced coins and most of the barbarian coinages were produced by tribes which had been settled in or seized part of the empire.

Their coinages follow the same general pattern. Imitations of imperial coins (usually in the name of the contemporary emperor, probably implying recognition of him) would be made for many years, and would then be replaced by a national coinage struck in the name of the king. Like all generalisations, this one has exceptions; the Burgundians and Suevi produced only imitative coins, while the Ostrogoths produced imitative gold, partially imitative silver, and regal copper all at the same time. It remains generally true, however, that imitative coinages were replaced by national ones, even though the change might take place at widely different times; the late sixth century for the Visigoths, but the late seventh century for the Lombards.

The first barbarian coinage seems to have been made by the Visigoths, who as a reward for helping the emperor Honorius against the Burgundian puppet emperor Jovinus (AD 411–13) in Gaul and against the Vandals in Spain were given a home in south-west France. There they probably produced a small series of imitative gold and silver coins in the name of Honorius. They soon extended their kingdom into Spain, although they lost most of France to the Franks in 507. For all this period they produced imitations of solidi and tremisses, particularly of the tremissis (**183**, an imitation of tremisses of Valentinian III such as **171**), but in the reign of Leovigild (AD 568–86) a regal Visigothic coinage began. These coins had a stylised portrait of the king, and were produced at some fifty mints throughout Spain. Their production continued until the Arab conquest of AD 711–714.

In fifth-century Spain, an imitative coinage of tremisses was also produced by the Suevi, at first in the name of Honorius, but mainly in the name of Valentinian III (AD 425–55: **184**, compare **171**), and with a distinctive treatment of the reverse design. Coinage may have diminished with their crushing defeat in 455, after which they were confined to a small area of northern Portugal, where they were finally destroyed in 585 by the Visigoths.

The Suevi had originally accompanied the Vandals to Spain, crossing the Rhine in 406 and then passing through France. After some years in Spain, the Vandals crossed to Africa in 429 and established a kindgom there, which was to last a century, surviving a major attempt to recapture Africa by the emperor Leo in 468 and falling only to Justinian in 533. It is not clear whether or not they produced any of their own coins before the reign of Gunthamund (484–96). Apart from a few silver coins cryptically dated to the fourth and fifth year of Carthage, however, it seems unlikely, and the subsequent production of their own coinage is probably to be explained by the death of the last western emperor, Julius Nepos, in 480. Their coins, which were produced in silver and bronze (their large bronze coins have already been mentioned), usually depict the king on the obverse (**185**, of Gunthamund) wearing the diadem, the symbol of the emperor, conspicuously avoided by other barbarian kings. This suggests that, with the end of the western empire, they assumed the privileges they had previously acknowledged as the prerogatives of the emperor, to wear a diadem and to strike coins in their own name.

In Italy, the last western emperor to rule was Romulus (475–76). He was deposed by an officer in the army, Odovacar, whose reign as 'king' over Italy lasted until 493 and who seems to have recognised the restored western emperor Julius Nepos, until Nepos's death in 480, and the eastern emperor Zeno. However, in 488 Zeno sent the Ostrogothic king Theoderic against him, and after a long struggle, during which Odovacar made coins in his own name (**180**), Italy became part of the Ostrogothic kingdom. The Ostrogothic kings thereafter made coins. Their gold and silver coins generally recognised the authority of the current emperor in Constantinople and added their own name usually only in the form of monogram (**182**, with the monogram of Theoderic at the end of the reverse legend). The bronze coinage they produced was, however, diverse in nature, sometimes with the head of the king on the obverse, but generally using the head of the personification of the mint city, for example FELIX RAVENNA. These coinages lasted until the reconquest of Italy by Justinian in 552.

The other main barbarian coinage of the fifth century was that of the Burgundians, allies of the Romans who had settled in the south of France, and who produced imitative coins from the reign of Gundobad (473–516), if not before. Most of these were solidi and tremisses in the name of the emperor Anastasius (with the addition of the king's monogram on the reverse: **186** has the monogram of king Sigismund). Additionally some very rare silver and bronze coins were also minted, whose mintmark LD suggests that the whole coinage came from LugDunum (Lyon). The Burgundians were finally conquered by the Franks in 534, who under their king Clovis (481–51) had come to rule most of modern France and part of Germany.

As well as the physical nature of the coins, the administrative basis of their production had also been changed by the political break-up of the empire. The idea of the "comitatensian mint" had gradually disappeared, particularly with the special relationship of the mint of Milan with the commander of the army, the Magister Militum. When Italy fell under Ostrogothic rule, minting was concentrated in Rome, although the king's residence remained at the imperial location of Ravenna. In Spain and France, the coinage was increasingly decentralised. As we have seen, the Visigothic regal coinage was produced at some fifty different mints, while in some areas the moneyers ceased to be state officials and were instead important private individuals. In the Frankish kingdom of the late sixth and early eighth century, much of the coinage did not bear the name of the king, or indeed the emperor, but simply that of the monetarius or moneyer: over a thousand of these have been recorded, working in a variety of places, like cities, royal estates or churches (for example 187, a tremissis of the moneyer Eligius, made at Paris). These changes symbolised not just the change of regime, but also the change in the type of society and its lack of strong centralised control.

By this stage the transformation of the Roman into the medieval world was well established, and it can be seen how medieval coinage grew in different ways from that of the Romans. In the central areas of the Mediterranean, the late Roman coinage system was taken over more or less intact by the new kingdoms, who produced solidi, tremisses, some silver and copious bronze coins in the traditional manner. Away from the centre, however, in Spain and northern Europe, only the Roman system of gold coinage was taken over (the exceptions are insignificant), and minting was largely confined to the solidus and, particularly, the tremissis. It was no doubt the difficulty of acquiring gold, most of which came from Roman or Byzantine subsidies, that led these kingdoms to concentrate on producing the smaller denomination, the tremissis, and to debase the gold coinage. Already by 458 the emperor Majorian allowed tax collectors to refuse "Gallic [= Visigothic?] solidi", since their "gold was reckoned at a lower value" (cuius aurum minore aestimatione taxatur: Nov. 7). "Gallic solidi" were notorious for their inferior quality over the succeeding hundred and fifty years (Gregory *Epist.* 6.10, of 595), and debasement continued until the Frankish coins, for instance, contained no more than about 30% of gold in the late seventh century. From that time, consequently, gold began to be replaced by silver, which became the predominant European coinage metal from the eighth century and set the scene for the coinage of the Middle Ages: gold "solidi" had been replaced by silver "pennies".

Appendix

Principal events and emperors

The Republic

		c.300	First silver coinage
281–75	Pyrrhic War		
264–41	First Punic War		
218–01	Second Punic (Hannibalic) War	c.212	Introduction of denarius
168	Conquest of Macedonia		
146	Annexation of Africa and sack of Corinth	c.141	Denarius retariffed at 16 asses
133	Acquisition of kingdom of Pergamum (= Province of Asia)		
112–06	War against Jugurtha in Africa	c.92	Papirian law (reduced asses, sestertii)
88–83	Sulla in east		
83–82	Sullan civil war	82–23	No bronze minted in Rome
67–63	Large commands of Pompey in east		
58–49	Caesar's Gallic command	58	Start of Romano-Syrian tetradrachms
49–45	Civil war of Pompey and Caesar		
44	Assassination of Caesar	46	Start of regular gold coinage
43	Triumvirate of Antony, Octavian and Lepidus		
42	Defeat of Brutus and Cassius		
36	Defeat of Sextus Pompey in Sicily	38–31	Debasement of Antony's silver
31	Defeat of Antony and Cleopatra at Actium		

Appendix: principal events and emperors

The Empire

31–AD14	Octavian (= Augustus)	c.23	Reform of bronze coinage at Rome
		c.15	Foundation of Lyon mint
		5BC	Reform of silver and bronze of Antioch
14–37	Tiberius	21	First Roman tetradrachms of Alexandria
37–41	Gaius ("Caligula")	c.40	End of civic coinage in the west
41–54	Claudius I		
54–68	Nero	64	Nero's reforms and debasement
68–69	Civil War		
69–79	Vespasian		
79–81	Titus		
81–96	Domitian	82	Reform of Domitian
96–98	Nerva		
98–117	Trajan	c.107	Debasement and withdrawal of earlier silver
117–38	Hadrian		
138–61	Antoninus Pius		Last semisses
161–80	Marcus Aurelius		
180–92	Commodus		
193–97	Civil War		
193–211	Septimius Severus	c.195	Debasement of silver
211–17	Caracalla	215	First "radiates"
217–18	Macrinus	217	Temporary improvement in silver fineness
218–22	Elagabalus		
222–35	Severus Alexander		
235–38	Maximinus		
238–44	Gordian III		Replacement of denarius by radiate
244–49	Philip		
249–51	Trajan Decius		Withdrawal of denarii
251–53	Trebonianus Gallus		
253–60	Valerian		Debasement of gold; collapse of silver; and end of bronze
253–68	Gallienus GAUL		
	260–69 Postumus		
	269–71 Victorinus		
268–70	Claudius II		
	271–74 Tetricus		
270–75	Aurelian		Restoration of gold fineness; introduction of "aurelianus" (XXI)
275–76	Tacitus		
276–82	Probus		
282–83	Carus		

Appendix: principal events and emperors

284–305	Diocletian and Maximian		Reforms of gold, silver and bronze; and of mint system
305–13	Maximinus		
306–12	Maxentius		
306–37	Constantine		Lower weight "solidus"
308–24	Licinius		
337–40	Constantine II		
337–50	Constans		
337–61	Constantius II	c.355–c.400	Plentiful silver
361–63	Julian		
363–64	Jovian		
364–75	Valentinian I	c.366	Reform of gold coinage
364–78	Valens		
367–83	Gratian		
379–95	Theodosius I	383	Introduction of tremissis

WEST		EAST		
395–423	Honorius	395–408	Arcadius	
423–25	Johannes	402–50	Theodosius II	
425–55	Valentinian III			
455–56	Avitus	450–57	Marcian	
457–61	Majorian	457–74	Leo	
461–65	Libius Severus			
467–72	Anthemius			
473–74	Glycerius			
474–75	Julius Nepos	474–91	Zeno	
			c.485	Introduction of larger bronzes in west
475–76	Romulus			
		491–518	Anastasius	
			498	Reform of Byzantine bronze coinage

List of illustrations

All the coins illustrated are in the British Museum collection, except for 141 and 145 (Vienna), 157 (Berlin) and 137 (Arras). 35 is in the Greek and Roman Department, British Museum. Copyright photographs are reproduced by kind permission of the British Museum, the Bodleian Library, Hirmer Verlag and Professor K.T. Erim.

164

List of illustrations

Additional illustrations

166

Index

Index